GRIGORI GRABOVOI

THE TEACHINGS OF GRIGORI GRABOVOI ABOUT GOD.

EAM Publishing
Edilma Angel Moyano
Contract: P527USA
That grants the right to use the brands GRABOVOI®
GRIGORI GRABOVOI®, for editions

Copyright © 2020 Dr. Grigori Grabovoi®
ISBN–13: 979 8602612912

Cover © D'har Services
ID:36480720©Agsandrew

- Serbia: GRIGORI GRABOVOI D.O.O., 2005, 2015.
Grigori Grabovoi © Grabovoi G.P., **28 February 2005,
24 March 2005, 12 August 2015 and 12 October
2015**

The text of the work was created for the first time by Grabovoi Grigori Petrovich during his seminars described above. When he creating the seminar, of the method of eternal development with the exact forecasting of the future events was applied. 100% validation of the forecasts made by Grabovoi G.P. has been proved by the protocols and testimonials, published in a 3-volume edition "Practice of Control. The Way of Salvation". When creating the text of the seminar, Grabovoi G.P. first had an accurate forecast of future events and then created a text teaching everyone eternal development, with due consideration for the specific events of the future, concerning every single person and the whole world.

THE METHODS OF REJUVENATION FOR ETERNAL LIFE

I

THE TEACHING OF GRIGORI GRABOVOI ABOUT GOD

REJUVENATION

February 28, 2005

Hello again!

The topic of my today's seminar is my Teaching "About God". Rejuvenation.

The topic, in this case, implies the identification of specific areas when rejuvenation is necessary for a human, for example, if we have such an action as, suppose, rational from the point of view of human health, or when a human personally makes a decision on rejuvenation due, for example, to personal reasons.

Therefore, the topic is divided into two parts, let's say: this is rejuvenation according to clinical indications, if it is necessary in order to restore the health of a human, and the second is a personal will. So, in the first part, I consider the process when it is necessary to consider the rejuvenation procedure as a structure of regeneration, that is, the restoration of tissue in a certain period of time of human. That is, a human is considered as, so to say, the global level of development of the whole World, as a development system with all connections, and a section, which specifically characterizes that at that moment a human had the most favorable health, is allocated, so to speak, of external and internal events. Therefore, rejuvenation still is a complex value in this case. And if we consider how, for example, God is doing from the point of view of rejuvenation procedure, then, for Him, in general, the process of control is such that we have the development, for example, of God's action such as the process of youth for Him, in principle, is a process of action. That is, it is an action to create a structure of youthfulness; to create the structure of old age is also an action, and so on. And so it is important to highlight the subjective reasons. That is, Soul of a human considers some period as a period, for example, a young one. And so it is important to highlight the subjective reasons. That is, the human Soul considers some period as a young period, for example. Therefore, in the structure of rejuvenation based on clinical reasons, the outlining of a spectrum of youth, after all, is a task of a subjective type. That is, a human at some period of time selects the phase of his personal youth.

For example, God perceives Himself young when He wants. That is, the concept of an old age does not exist for God in principle. He can perceive any time interval, for example, as an interval of a young state. Therefore, it is a special technology of the combination of certain signs of state for God, for example, to differentiate what youth or, suppose, old age is for Him. And therefore, it turns out that for a human, in order to rejuvenate, it is also necessary to think and consider exactly the structure when he had the most optimal qualities from the point of view of that manifestation, what is called, for example, youth. Therefore, the first phase is the selection of the structure of control for the young state precisely for clinical reasons. That is, a human must be healthy, to restore, let's suppose, health; and, the second, is the use of the highlighted segment of information in order to draw this segment of information to the present time. Then the transformation phase comes, that is, the response of the body to this state, and the adaptation phase.

And so, the longest one, or the phase that has a certain pressure wave is precisely the phase of adaptation. Because, both the first and the second systems, when a human outlines a phase in the way God does, in general it is not difficult. It is enough to recall two or three useful concepts from the structure of youth. So, the adaptation phase in the organism is a natural state: the organism was young. In this regard, it turns out that there is nothing unnatural about this, but it is the adaptation phase to the current time, where there is a change of social, physical, and some informative events. This is the main position in this control. Therefore, if we assume that the first two phases take a thousandth of a percent: the outlining and, in general, the attraction to the structure of the current time – then mainly, in the structure of rejuvenation, it is necessary to deal with clinical indications specifically when it comes to recovery, I again focus attention, sometimes to normalize some events with the aim of getting health, and so on.

* * *

For example, in the technologies of eternal life it is necessary to be able to periodically rejuvenate at the will of the human. And, in this regard, if, suppose, we consider such a structure as, for example, resurrection, then it turns out, the work, in this case, with the tissue should go in a fairly direct way to achieve the desired age of control, and so on. Therefore, in principle, the technology of fixing a certain image in a more general way, for example, from the point of view of technology, for example, of eternal development, we are talking about the fact that we select a segment of time, and carry out the control so that we say that at this time we have such an age, yes?.. and such characteristics of health. And when we use this in order to have exactly the characteristics of health, provided that the first level is the level that is still the main which stands out in control: this is the need for highlighting the structure of human non dying in the technologies of eternal development, that is, a human should not die under any conditions. Therefore, it turns out that from the point of view of the onset of old age, this is also, in general, a rather important technological level for the technology of eternal development.

And here it is precisely the adaptation to the structure of external events that is done in the same way as God does. That is, overcoming sometimes literally instantly, it can be done, for example, by some analyzing through the structure of diagnostics of the Soul, perceiving some better, let's say, state, which we define as the structure of youth, without taking into account specifically external and internal parameters. This is, in general, a state fairly clear to any human from the point of view of information. If we consider how a human, for example, thinks, what is the structure of mind, for example, in the center of action, then this is just the same structure of optimality of a certain youth.

What is youth in the informative understanding? Accomplishment of some kind of close or periodically close actions which are rather new, initial actions, which then, for example, may not end. In principle, this is the technology of eternal development in subjective perception. Therefore, in this case, when we consider the adaptive function, when the human has already taken the control, sent the optical phase to himself. And then the adaptation of the organism to current events begins. This is where the main tasks in control arise.

The first task is to withdraw the structure of the young state, so let's say, which is controlled as a state integrated with the organism into the structure of infinite development. If you manage to bring out immediately, the human rejuvenates quickly enough. It is as if by one impulse you have brought it into the structure of infinite development and received the Light from infinity to your side. Then the adaptation takes place very quickly. If somewhere, in some integration of control, it turns out that we, as it were, have got an additional node of control, that is, an additional connection, which may be such that at the moment of rejuvenation the person begins to think how he will be perceived by others, or, what age, how it will generally look subjectively, that is, some subjective thoughts, often these are the thoughts that are not fundamental, as a rule, and they arise in the first level of control, then the main level of blocking the adaptation exactly of the structure of youth to the organism arises here. In fact, although this may lead to physiological recovery, the sort of visual manifestation of the structure, so to speak, of the young state begins to slow down in time due to some kind of pictures appearing in the control.

In order to speed up the control, it is necessary to circumvent the structure, kind of periodic or systemic thinking, where similar questions arise, for example, how to rejuvenate for a specific time? Then it turns out that the main task of control is actually rejuvenation for a specific time. Then the whole complex of tasks disappears. For example, a human rejuvenated for five, ten, or fifteen years; he knows approximately about the reaction of others to himself and understands that if he, for example, needs it, it is necessary to rejuvenate for such age somehow. Perhaps, in order just to rejuvenate for clinical reasons, that is, to improve your health, rejuvenation, for example, for a month or for a second is enough, to make, for example, a push phase at that second. That is, it is enough to make as if an integration in time minus one second, and, it turns out, due to just the elasticity of the tissue, because it is, after all, in general, the control of the tissue systems, the organism becomes normalized. That is exactly when we talk about rejuvenation for a clinical reasons of a human - that is, he may not be sick, generally speaking, but he just wants to be healthier, - this is also, in general, as one of the features of, let's say, of conditionally clinical reasons, because in principle I am now talking about the fact that, through this structure, one can be cured from some problems or, in principle, to cure serious diseases through the structure of rejuvenation. This is what I call "for clinical reasons." And while the property of time in this case is very simple. If we bring the organism into the state, in which it as if recalls the natural level, where there was no illness, in fact, and moreover from the point of view of future events, we throw it in the structure of future events, even without working often with the past element of time, then we get, in general, just a normal state of health. Therefore, it turns out that this is on condition that health, generally speaking, can be normal anyway. But this procedure can be applied as if to prevent any problems, can be used to get rid of environmentally harmful systems of influence.

What is youth? This is a certain normalized primary environment. And if there is a radiation effect or toxicological effect, you can simply bring the organism out of the phase of this effect due to the fact that the adaptive functions of the state of youth are high as it is considered so. Although this a quite conditional state for God. For God, there is just an adaptation and control function. Therefore, we, simply speaking, conditionally name youth the state of increased adaptation. And we make the tissue less informative loaded from the point of view of previous development systems, or from the point of view of receiving information.

Ultimately, we have to make the cell infinitely perceiving any information system. Then it turns out, the movement in the structure of time or structure of youth is a personal level, in general. Human looks like as he wants to look, for example. And, based on these clinical norms, let's say, the norms of physiological indicators, we can fully assume that this is in general, the means for normalization of the organism, well, including the healthy one, from the point of view of normalization, for example, according to environmental indicators, ability of the organism to react to some situation. Suppose a person has some complicated situation. Then it is easier to enter the state of a young integration into reality and react as if in a younger way, so to speak, well, in quotes. For example, you need to increase the emotional background of control. You enter the state and you just work informatively. At the same time, you can be calm, but you have entered the state, for example, of the young level and worked based on the emotional type, that is, you conducted the main control through the emotion. Then it turns out that you basically worked as a young person who works at this time, and, for example, in a similar way, Because the Collective Consciousness in general, contains certain signs, as if of the emotional level of youth, a certain level of action in terms of how a young person acts, and so on. And therefore, in principle, we say that we know this information, for example, or approximately know who was, for example, in the state of youth, being an ordinary, the same person as he would be later, then he may have no difference. But we believe that we can use conditional values that relate to the concept of youth. Well, in this case, that is, we can assume that there are certain states in youth that characterize precisely the concept of youth according to the emotional, psychological plan, and in accordance with the control plan. And in this regard, we have, in principle, quite a large choice of control. What is another characteristic of the young state? From the point of view of a younger state, you have overcome, for example, a certain level of control, for example, you have overcome some systems that were in front of you. So you have experience to overcome. So you can overcome. And, if you take the usual core construction and insert everything as if in a model solution – now there is a problem and to make some kind of universal decision, perhaps, an action – you just take the shape and impose it on the structure of control. It turns out, you always overcome. That is, the state of youth is a state of obligatory overcoming of the problem, it turns out that it is logically simple. And, by the way, it is so in terms of control.

From the point of view of a personal control plan, for example, a human, having no clinical indications, he is healthy, he has no environmental problems, and he has decided just to rejuvenate at his own wish? This is the next level of control. Then the question arises, why does he need it? Well, for example, an aesthetic level or a personal level, if a person thinks that with a sort of increase of age, of age characteristics, he, on the contrary, has his social status, and so on. That is, this is also, in general, such a level, as of a systematic type. But here there is one nuance that, from the point of view of personal choice, towards development, for example, of aging processes, so to speak, or old age, the structure is very complicated in control. That is, for example, if a person has chosen the level of rejuvenation, then it is an adaptive level to reality, that is, he should be, for example, of a certain age, right? In this case, we are still talking about a broader integration of concepts, because human has the tasks of the Soul, the tasks for personal development. If he, for example, a professor, Ph.D. believes that he must be at some age, at least maybe a little older than sixteen years at least. Therefore, it turns out that there are some levels, a sort of subjective levels, as if certain phases of the Collective Consciousness, which nevertheless influence the control system, it is as if an external control. If it is in the case of the control on rejuvenation according to clinical reasons for recovery, nothing should impact at all here in principle – a person decided to improve his health, he has rejuvenated, and there are no other criteria, because health is the absolute norm of any control - then in the case of a personal choice a lot of nuances of such type arise. In this case it can either lead to recovery... Then the question arises - for healthy people this is a rather complicated construction, that is, you can just be healthy - why be young, right?.. for example, what's the difference? A healthy person still does the same things. Well, he, as it were, is ready to work in any control status.

And here comes the nuance from the point of view of technologies of eternal development. In this case, the root of the situation itself is that when we consider, for example, the structure of resurrection, the structure of the restoration of a certain flower, some blade of grass in infinite development, God can restore everything, because He sees everything simultaneously in real time. This is where the context of personal and quick decision making arises. That is, the rejuvenation by personal choice is still a quick choice of this sort of solution. Suppose, for God, to restore some blade of grass, which is somewhere very far in time for Him, means to develop it very quickly into this time, right?.. And it will grow now somewhere here. That is, it turns out that – that is at this time, for example, and this is the level of a very quick decision - in order to rejuvenate according to a personal plan, you should make a quick decision. At the same time, in this case, the concept of rejuvenation sometimes has a subjective control system. For example, a person takes an exam, but he studied the topic of the ticket before, right?.. Then it turns out that he can use this system in order just to be in this state when he has learned the topic of this ticket. Well, this is a sort of tool of memory training, or a tool of sort of to know everything without overloading memory, right?.. That is, it turns out that, on the basis of this, it is like a technological method of application of this process. And it turns out that, based on this, we can, in principle, have access to this information, if we extrapolate our Consciousness, the Consciousness segment into the structure of writing a book in general, and try to understand the emotional structure in terms of age.

Because the understanding of the age and of the way, which the author followed, is also a system of learning. To understand the structure of control, it is enough to know the author, right? And then it turns out that you should know his age characteristics. It is often easier to understand the author by age, it is enough to see the structure of age, and you understand what he wrote. And it turns out that, based on this, it is possible in principle just to take and read information, in the form of reading the texts technologically, to study something for a long time. That is, in general, this is the system of access to the information of control of this process. And when you begin to set tasks, then we will move on to technological methods, then the rejuvenation method in this case – here I give the methodological plan to a certain extent, because, after all, it is the system of a personal choice in this case, it, in general, makes the task more generalized – and then it is necessary to normalize in terms of the methodological plan. So, by the method of rejuvenation based on personal choice: a person just decided to rejuvenate, for example, the method is as follows.

So, the first method is that you need to perceive yourself, so to speak, in the infinite future as the structure of the manifestation of the external world, that is, you look into infinity, but you see an increasing level of yourself. At first these are informative signs. By the way, this is a very strong level of development of clairvoyance to control the situation around you. And when you begin to see a sort of your informative plan, you begin to understand how you generally work at the level of information. Suppose, if you perceive some kind of information object, then it turns out that here you can understand how the information develops in relation to you, that is, in general, how you work in information, how you look at information. And when you begin to develop this system, it is only your personal, a sort of original image, the one that was originally created by God or conceived by God, so to speak, shows how you work with information in this level of your thinking. And when you begin to trace your own connections that come from you, then, naturally, the whole system is controllable. So, it turns out that this method enables you to keep track of all your own connections, which you practically build independently, that is, track your own channels, so to speak, or optical systems of control. So, you can have access to any of your own tissue in control, in information. That is, it turns out, you do not have to touch your tissue system directly, but in integration with the entire system of connection of the whole world you can clearly correct the system. And you will be at that age, which age you will have fixated. And here there is such an axiomatic sign. The axiom is as follows: no matter how much you do the additional control except for the first one, first, a sort of the first wave, all the following control will always go to you personally. And you will again have to do the control in the next status. That is, it is impossible to work constantly on one system, kind of a coordinate one. Well, as they say - it is impossible to enter the same water twice, and so on. That is, it means that in this case we are talking about the primary status of the primary level of living. What is generally the aging process or, for example, the process of youth - this is a process of changing some information. And in principle, the task of rejuvenation is the ability, in the current time, to create a system practically of the same type, which you have already used, in general, with other structures of control, that is, in general, the form that is known for you. And we actually want to use this form for the second time.

Every element of information is equal for God. Therefore, the transition to this form is the primary phenomenon for Him. In this case you have to understand God. This is, what He wanted for you in this level, when He gave you the next level of development, for example, in the direction of aging, in the direction of what exists in Collective Consciousness actually, what is considered to be aging, for example. And then it turns out that if we look at the primary form and want to understand why we are going along the common phase of the Collective Consciousness, why do we need it at all. Well, you can be young, for example, eternal time or at some age. Why are we going the same way as everyone and, for example, in order not to differ, right? Or what do we need to have, when we have signs of aging, what do we want in this world generally? That is, human always chooses personally. And then it turns out that from the point of view of God, it is still a collective action.

In order to redefine the structure, a human can act as God does. He can redefine the structure for himself and then act individually, but in order to reflect it to others he has to teach others. And as soon as the process of teaching others by one human becomes more or less systemic, that is, he transfers more knowledge, either implicit or explicit, suppose, lectures knowledge, or at least is doing mentally, or he wishes youth for them, he enters more the structure of the control of this process by his will.

And then the next axiom arises, in order to rejuvenate, for example, the maximum number of the population or the entire globe, for example, for a while, for a second, it is necessary to ensure that everyone gets for this second – well, this is roughly within this time – the knowledge, which is from the beginning of their organization to this second, that is, actually the vector of rejuvenation, that is, a change in the structure of the entire reality. Well, any event for God is equal: that is, all the preceding events and all the following, right? Therefore, to rejuvenate basically for ten years or for a second is the same task of control. And although we are making this second equal, we equate it to all the previous development in order to change some event in the world, suppose, then it turns out that we have such a level of control that all previous work seems to be aimed at changing a particular event. That is, we have to equate what we want to solve in the next second, with what we have, for example, as a task of our own development in general. That is, one local action is equalized to the choice of the whole goal, so let's say, of the human development up to this time. And when we start to equalize, in principle, it's all the same for God. All the same, God acts once, but He acts forever. And a one-time action or an eternal action are all the same for Him, generally speaking. That is, we are just entering the same system of control. And it turns out that when we enter it, an adaptation process of the following type occurs, that a large enough mass of time, let's say, the mass of events begins to act in a wavelike manner, practically it is directly felt as if informationally, although it is often felt even on the physical level as a kind of wave that is near the body, like, for example, a person who is swimming in some very salty water - this is a kind of external wave. And this whole spectral level shows that all the next reality, it often has, as it were, a level that is defined incorrectly.

That is, you are getting closer to the structure of building the world and events. And that's when you start to see that building the world and events at the current moment is determined by the fact that, at the level of any level of control of any external even system, you are sure that you have eternal development, that is, the confidence arises from the level of earlier decisions. That is, you decided to rejuvenate earlier, you did actions earlier, and then any information suggests that this is achievable, even, by the way, it may be some kind of pressure information, it may require some kind of reaction. That is, it is not always some kind of favorable information, but at a certain level of knowledge you clearly understand that you will reach that system that you need, that is, at least even in the near-cellular space. It is very important in the structure of my lecture systems that the near-cellular space begins to work as the structure of reserve of the cell itself in the structure of control. That is, it is not necessary to see this information as the structure of the cell itself of a human, for example. Let's consider, for example, a cell of the heart. The cell of the heart is a completely objective information, which has, for example, this information, because you thought about it earlier, and you have this information in this cell as the history of your development. But in this system, near-cellular information has the same status. That is, you actually accept this information and have the same status of development of an event plan. So, your events are very reserved, it turns out, in terms of power, so to say. That is any action first gets to the near-informative level, that is, not to your cellular level, but to the information about you. That is, you consciously transfer any action to the informative level of control. So, in order to reach you from outside as if, for example, in some negative perspective, first it is necessary to overcome a virtually comparable structure. And it turns out, if we reserve this level of control several times, - for example, we can do it as much as we want, depending on the time, - then it turns out that the coming of a signal, perhaps, of a negative type to you is much more complicated.

Then it turns out that we fall into approximately the same structure of development as God does. He created everything, but nothing can be sort of radically negative for Him, from the point of view of affecting Him, right? He can live through personally, make decisions and somehow react in His own way, but it is not possible to get Him, God. And it turns out that from the point of view of this process He is in the level, that any system of action on Him or an appeal is the level of just such an informative action, but the appeal is, generally speaking, the youth, that is, the level of youth. If we want to realize the level of youth for ourselves, then we have to appeal to God in the place where He Himself is young, and God, He is young everywhere. There is no concept of age as such. If you think about it, for example, the age of God, that is, to ask such a question right now, what is His age? Then it turns out, we can see the age, if we think, we say that it is the age which God Himself considers at the moment. He determined such an age for himself. So, in general, we see Him the same way, can see visually, visually only in principle.

What is the other age criterion? Why does God need to be in the physical body of human? To ensure that the age, at least, is visible, and because it is possible to transfer knowledge even through age category. For example, if God acts as a child, right? He grows, then, accordingly, the level of knowledge transfer goes to children, for example, it is further, and so on. From a certain age, for example, from sixteen years old, God can transfer knowledge more widely, as soon as he received the passport, and so on. That is, the criteria for the transfer of knowledge are the same, in principle, as when a human transfers knowledge to another human or to all people at once. And therefore, in this system namely of macro-salvation, let's say, of the salvation of everyone from the level of cognition or the actions of rejuvenation, we can see that it is exactly the integrated Consciousness of God and human in the structure of absence of time, or in the structure of eternal youth, so to be called, this state is the level of multiple backup, in fact, for the control of external information. In the end, or, let's say, at the control level, it looks like this: all external information is controlled to a certain level as if it reaches some criteria and starts to be controlled, for example, further than the physical body. And now the information of a more or completely favorable sense, or at least a more favorable sense, approaches the physical body, when the process, for example, is brought to the level of improvement of the model of the primary identification of information of an unfavorable sense, aligning the lines of the vector controls and obtaining favorable information. Although it may be so for a human, or for a human Soul, that some situations are organized by him, in general, it seems perhaps for external systems, that this is unfavorable, except for completely negative cases, which are clear that they are negative anyway, any other systems may be conditional, they are not necessarily negative for this individual. Perhaps this is the way of some kind of development, and so on.

And therefore, differentiation in a complex system of completely linear systems takes place according to the laws, first of all, for example, the health norm, then development towards the technology of eternal development, some very specific norms, it is clear that they must be kept, if the contour of control is now following them, then it is already clear this should be corrected. And in all other cases, the question of action arises. That's when we understand the root of the action, for example, God created the whole world, but what is the root level for Him?.. or, let's say, what is internally maximally developed, we may say, by some sacramental moment in this situation?.. what does He perceive as the essence of the situation in the whole world? At the same time, with all that, for Him, both towards plus infinity or towards minus infinity is all the same for Him. Whereas God identifies for Himself exactly the essence of this process, which is the essence of this process for Him. It turns out that for God the essence of this process is what He laid, for example, from the point of view of eternal development, for example, the eternal development of mankind or a particular person. And that's when He sees that He is developing normally in this plan, He, God, is realizing His essence at this moment. Then what is the same thing for human in this case, or, let's say, a similar one, in general?

If a human see that he has given knowledge to another one, or has been able to show development to infinity, at least he has given knowledge about eternal development, it means he has somehow realized himself as well. Well, first of all, a simple technological principle. By giving knowledge to another one, he actually is getting the experience of development, and has got it back to himself, and this happens almost instantly for human. It is only necessary to give knowledge and, although the other person begins to develop in the direction of infinity, the one, who has transferred the knowledge, immediately receives the whole experience of the development of this person in infinity. That is, these are incomparable in volume systems of control. For example, you can give one method of development, and get in response what the person who has learned this method will receive in his infinite development. But, generally speaking, God acts the same way. In order to develop the system of the world to infinity, for this He needs, at the boundary point of each phenomenon, - for example, we consider that the whole world is a sphere, - to ensure that it develops infinitely, every point of the sphere should give infinite development to the entire outside world, it's a geometric model. That is why it turns out that when you give knowledge about eternal development, you actually get an infinite level of knowledge of the entire external world.

And God does the same. He should know the whole outside world from the point of view of logic, of human logic of development. There is, of course, the logic of development from God, when God just sees everything at once, and He does not have such tasks, that is, it is simple for Him: He does everything and sees everything at once. This is another system of cognition. And from the point of view of logic, He should see the logical connection, from the point of view, so to speak, of such logic, which is considered the logic of the expediency of a process, or the logic, for example, of a possibility in the development of the process. And that's when we combine the logic of God, for example, when everything is at once for Him, and the logic that is close to the logic of the development of the physical environment, which people observed, it turns out that here, in the center, a very simple picture appears, in principle, as if such a methodological one, like a simple rejuvenation method. So, the human is just opposite the Physical Body of God and this glow that comes from God rejuvenates human. God and human have the same perception status of two objects, of two systems. And when you see this silver Light, that is, the whole outer and inner world appears. And the formation of the inner world sets, as it were, more the next task. Because your next tasks are such that what is set before you as the next task, it is considered as a task in communion with God, that is, an exact task, where you communicate. After all, dialogue is communication. You are not imposed anything in a dialogue, in communication, or, for example, in contact with God, you implement your own task. And it arises inside the heart, or inside the physical body and begins to develop. That's why human needs physical body: to show that he is free. He has personally produced his own task from his physical body, and he is solving it himself, it turns out. That is, it turns out that human has nothing but a personal task, in principle, from this point of view at the moment of contact with God.

And when you begin to transfer such a principle of contact to another human, you understand very clearly that you instantly, in fact, transfer any of your knowledge that you possess to other people. You just need to know it and understand how you do it technologically. And when you are already learning and already know how to transfer, at least the main amount in exactly this way, in such real time as God transfers to you, then in principle you fixate the structure of your development from the point view of time, let's say, of age. Here you can vary. That's when the transfer goes on continuously, just as you look at the world, when you can transfer this knowledge to other people, for example, of eternal development, creative knowledge, then here you can easily move age wherever you want, in principle, it is not a problem any longer. Then you do the control, then your actions are justified. That is, you can say that you are doing control in order to make another person understand more. For example, there is a person in the classroom who needs that you look younger, then please rejuvenate and transfer knowledge, so that he can understand better. And it turns out that the rationality, as it were, falls into the structure of the action, well, maybe there should be some kind of integrated age that is clear to everyone, right? So, from the point of view of God, no matter what the age of God may be, it should still be logically clear to everyone. But, for example, from the point of view of a child, if God does not look the way he wants, that is, it is better for the child that God looks, at least as such an average level human. That is not any one there with a beard, which, for example, can frighten the child, at least God should not frighten off the child in this case. And it turns out that there is some kind of average image, which is a mode of action. And, in this image, like through a certain system of labyrinths of a certain level of overcoming, you can see that in the rings or in the way of the Collective Consciousness, where there is a certain integrated image; it serves for something.

That is, what is the meaning of age or some average qualities of a human at a certain age - well, to serve some task or perform some task. A school teacher should be of some age, for example, as children consider. If a teacher is the same age as schoolchildren, well, this, in general, complicates the transfer of knowledge at least, although, in general, it is permissible. But if we see that the teacher is of an earlier age, then the question arises, how it is if he finished several classes? Why does he teach, for example, older children? Well, that is, if we begin to dive into the logic of these tasks, we begin to find out what age is for Consciousness, then the most common sense will react for us, we will need some time for thinking which it is, in general. We can only think within that time that provides global safety of development. Well, it is as any common sense is aimed at realizing the structure, for example, of macro-salvation to begin with. If you reason for a very long time, develop some lines of development, completely artificial, then you can, in general, get away from the control system far enough.

From this point of view, there is the next level of control exactly in rejuvenation, this is to do concrete actions like God does. At the same time, no one is forbidden to think on anything. But what for, for example, there is sort of axiomatic sign of the Collective Consciousness, when we get, in fact, certain norms, inherent in society, in the social plan of governance, or in the political plan of governance? When we see that these systems are integrated to perform some tasks, we can technologically circumvent these systems. For example, if it is established that a teacher must be of such and such age in school, in secondary school, then it is necessary to see what his image gives for general development or for eternal life in this case. If you are tracing these lines, then you can become younger, if you are a teacher, for example, in high school, and start working just technologically, that is, you will be compensating for the lines of social status just by control. If we are talking about any other person, - for example, he is a leader or he has any kind of functional system of management in society - then you should just compensate for what is required from the particular person at that age, just as if compensate, or to replace with the actual control. That is, to work, so to speak, intellectually, to consider what the Collective Consciousness does, for example, at this moment for this person. There are also the tasks of God there, and his personal task, that he achieves something at some age. But it is still necessary to keep track of the lines here, what many people thought about him, that he would be doing something at that age, for example, typical of an adult person. Then it turns out, it is still necessary to track down the thoughts that seemed to be preparing him for this state, that is, the thoughts of relatives, friends, acquaintances, generally speaking, just the thoughts of strangers who see the person on the sidewalk, just random people. And when you start to analyze, it turns out, just random do not exist. Any point of view is an objective point of view the same as of any other person. If a relative has, for longtime, imagined you as an adult, for example, there you are, finally, you have become an adult. And then you, as if from his point of view, are prolonging the path of your development, gaining age, and a person who could just happen to see you somewhere at a certain age, right? Then a long way of building up the thought-forms of relatives and the only look for God is one and the same thing.

And then you need to consider, you can compensate for all development systems. But if you do not consider a single glance in relation to yourself, you will have to work for a long time near the same system. That is why you need to be able to develop a spiritual vision in the structure of any signal that relates to your age. Therefore, the following axiomatic-methodological principle arises, so to say, where the axiom is that this is exactly the nature of information, so to say, and the methodology is an action in this nature, that when controlling for rejuvenation, when it is done by personal desire, it is necessary to consider how much your desires correspond to the external point of view, even if it was completely one-off and completely random. And when, for example, you start to look at these elements of control - you walked somewhere along the street, a person looked at you, he fixed the reality at a particular point, right?.. Then it turns out, in order to make this reality mobile, it is necessary for this person to agree actually that you, for example, are even younger at the moment. Since this is unusual for him, isn't it? .. at that moment. And so there is a question, how to convince him in absentia? That is why I think it is necessary to develop namely the system, including the transfer of educational technologies in a direct, as it were, correspondence (in absentia) way. Because here it turns out that you can transfer the structure of knowledge to this person that it is possible, in general, that this it is about just regulating the communication systems in the world and that's all. And you become as if younger in his perception at this point in time. Then here there are specific principles for the transfer of this information. As soon as you find it, it is not necessary to find the specific person, you just find the signals that exist in your information of development and transmit through these signals to the unified, single image of person to the level of the right hand. You can mentally place the sphere of eternal development there and let this sphere, in the physical body of the person as such, begin just to diverge and actually rejuvenate him. That is the peculiarity of this situation. That is, if you have found a methodology for rejuvenating another person by your action, you are actually rejuvenating yourself.

Then you do not need to explain. He is personally convinced that he is just becoming younger. And when you have rejuvenated all the systems of connections around you, say, from the point of view of people, for example, or you have made it so that the plants have been green for longer time, the animals are younger, and so on, in this case you have come to the same way as God acts. That is, you actually create, around yourself, a certain system of normalized time, at the moment of which all processes are balanced and there is no, for example, the structure of old age. That is, there is a normalized time, which is characterized precisely by the concept of youth. Then this time can be increased, it is possible, as it were, to develop it, it is possible to attribute some characteristics to it, or attribute some specific level of youth, a specific age, for example, and, going out by this time, create this field accessible for the intensive level of control. As soon as you enter this field of control – that is it. You have entered the rejuvenation structure and are there. The more time you are in this system, the more you rejuvenate.

With this I finish today's seminar.
Thank you very much for your attention.

Author's seminar held by Grigori P. Grabovoi

II
THE TEACHING OF GRIGORI GRABOVOI ABOUT GOD. REJUVENATION BY ETERNITY.

March 24, 2005

Hello.

The topic of my today's seminar is my Teaching "About God". Rejuvenation by Eternity.

In this topic, I show how a human who has control in the field of Eternity uses these concepts and technologies in order to rejuvenate and improve his health. And in principle, the situation here is such that, to a greater degree, it is the context of healing through rejuvenation technologies that will be expressed when it comes to control through Eternity.

In order to introduce this procedure of action on the given topic into control, it is necessary to do so that when you are considering, for example, some infinite level of control, some infinite horizon, you can actually use this concentration of optics in order to have a more favorable health or, simply put, just to improve your health, and to be able to use this concentration actually of the optical environment to ensure that health is always normal. Because in the technologies of eternal development according to my Teachings, we actually have the need of the following type, that any level of control that exists, for example, some horizon, some real object, a sea, suppose, a river – all these objects have to give human energy in fact. That is any visual object has to give a certain action. That is in fact this is about just transferring the perception into the action. And in connection to this - when we already have, for example such level that your perception prior to your looking somewhere gives you the level of actions, that is a transfer to some muscle movement, a transfer to the norm of the health, then actually you receive the health simply due to the fact that you live, let's say so. And we get a sort of vicious circle in the sense that you have almost eternal health just because you are created.

And here you can see how God initially created human and gave him the opportunity, in fact, due to the fact of creation, to have practically infinite development. Generally speaking, here, we have a very interesting point. In these terms we can see how human is created eternal and healthy, sort of healthy forever. And by the way, here is a simple example in this regard. Here is some horizon, right?... for example, you just look at the horizon, then you imagine this horizon in your mind. There is some point of control, and you choose a structure inside this point, a structure of a sort of you own "I", that is you see where you were created as an infinite one, where you were created as eternal one.

And finally you are moving on to how God really created you, that is, your movement and contact with God at some point – in fact this is the level which is not perceived by the level of the first wave of Consciousness. That is, it is so natural that you understand that you yourself always contacted with God in this very level.

Now, if you ask a person where he always keeps in touch with God, for example, it turns out that it is exactly in the structure of eternal development. Because there is a simple, even logical method: in infinite development, there are a lot of some elements that are completely different, right?... a sort of accidental, and there is an action of God there. The action of God is expressed where the infinite level of development practically exists.

And, for example, you can see, it turns out, that there is a different level of perception even for different regions, let's say, a different level of action of people, namely at the level of primary levels of perception. There is such a plan, sort of, in the perception of human, that in one region this very horizon, some infinite information, is closer, in a geographic region, and in another region this information is farther. For example, in the Far North, the region is perceived in such a way in a control, that this horizon line at the level, for example, of the action of the Spirit is further away, it's simply just geographically further.

And it turns out that if we want to do the same as God does, right?.. for example, anyway He has, for all, a universal action for the universal level of human, for every human – well, it is eternally living person, if we consider this level, then the perception should be the same everywhere, that is, people, generally speaking, should live well the same way everywhere, it turns out, it is good to. Such a social level arises here. And when we start proceeding from here, from the level of further control of reality, it turns out that reality itself is some rather mobile, controllable value, and, generally speaking, this horizon of perception can be moved closer to yourself. That is, God created the World in such a way that the World develops dynamically depending also on your perception system.

If we want, for example, to grow the vineyard of a higher quality, and get the harvest that is more appropriate for your goals, then it turns out that we can actually create such a level of action by control that we are actually creating as a platform, that is, the very ground of control as well as separate sort of segments. That is, we create, for example, the bush itself, where there are grapes, and at the same time we can consider this block as if separately from the whole World, so let's say, that is, to build it independently, and the concentration of your Consciousness increases in this level.

And if we consider the action in relation to a human in the same way, it turns out that the action here is, in principle, completely different. Man, always exists independently of the action directed to him. That is, we come to the action of God towards human. That is, the creation of a healthy human is a certain absolute value. If we, well in any other... As I, have gave an example here, we can consider some element of reality as an autonomous element, as it were, right?... for example some bush of grapes, and act as if from the outside, as for human, we always act in relation to what is the essence of human, which exists everywhere.

And here we have come to the conclusion that the essence of human, moreover, of every human, as if of some unified human, exists practically in any reality. The same as God does. Now, if you want to remember a relative, for example, or some familiar person, or just a person, well, maybe you only once saw him once, right?.. maybe in early childhood, and then you immediately understand his presence as if everywhere. This is, in principle, such a level of perception in human. That is, another person is perceived as a structure that is almost omnipresent, so to speak, in action related to you, right?... That is, the human acts in relation to another human as a structure that exists everywhere.

This level is the center of creation of human in the spiritual plan of God. That is, the Spirit of God acts in the same way as the Soul of human precisely into the area of remote action. Well, like an axiom in this case. It is possible to see at light-optics and see how the interaction of the Spirit of human and the Soul of God takes place, or, for example, the interaction of the Soul of God and the body of human. And here it is specifically the direct way to recovery, where you begin actually to correlate, that is, to think simultaneously with God and with other people, for example, in terms of eternal development.

If you consider, for example, how human in general thinks so that his thoughts were similar. All people have different thoughts, but these are precisely the thoughts in the direction of eternal development, they may be of the same type. This is very important. That is, in the eternal development a thought can be ... For example, in eternal development, when human thinks for a long time, having studied some phenomenon of reality, for example, a bush of some plant, in general, for example, a bush which can be in the form, for example, of your further action – the bush of a plant, - then all people who think up something, as it were, at an infinite level, begin to increase the glow of their every thought to some particular plant, and we get that any element of reality in an infinite level, is very pronounced in the cumulative action of all people.

That is, what is exactly, so to say, the difference even in the infinite development, when people have been thinking up for infinite time, it turns out that they have just health, because each element of reality due to their thinking becomes, in fact, eternal, just due to their thinking. And when a human begins to understand this, he sees how God created even further and the primary thought of human as well. After all, in fact, there is a rather important moment, that there is a person, and where he expressed his thought for the first time, for example.

Now, if you set the question like this: God created human, but how did the first thought come to the mind, so to speak, of human, or it just appeared from somewhere. And here, it turns out, that this first thought, so let's say, the first level actually of perception, that is, the first thought is what the human perceived first. And, then the question is, by what he perceived.

Well, in order for a human just to be healthy, to recover from the initial level, as if of his primary creation, he should see that he perceived it with his body. That is, he should consider the body as a system of perception, in fact, as the level of the action of God. Then the body is not separated from the action of God, that is, in fact, the Body of God and the body of human have the same structure at the level of molecules, at the level of cells, and so on. And, in general, it will be enough in this plan just to see virtually infinity due to the spiritual action, just due to the work of the Spirit, that is, the Spirit is infinite, then it turns out that the body is also eternal in this level of control.

When a human comes to such level, it is clear that exactly the fact, for example, of rejuvenation of human is just like a kind of correlation with the primary level of Consciousness. After all, the easiest way to rejuvenate when he, human, sees precisely the level of creation by God, that's when God created human, and it is enough to enter this glow. It is geometrically close enough, literally where I show it with my hand, this optics is expressed in this place in relation to a human, vertical line is literally in 15 centimeters from the human body – this is creation by God, and external perception that is 5 centimeters somewhere to the right. And that's all. Just fix Consciousness at this point and see how God initially created human - this is actually the generation of rejuvenation, that is, it is the very act of rejuvenation, and, in general, it is the generation of a certain environment around.

That's what is important in this structure of rejuvenation through healing, right?.. it is necessary to see that the external environment is also changing.

Well, let's take some material object, any object, and in principle we should do so that a person has rejuvenated, and then it turns out that based on the level of the tasks, we have to see how the elements of reality interact with that person who is rejuvenated. That is, in fact, we have to unwind also backwards in time any nearby element of the material world, because with the real rejuvenation, some elements still become of the same type. That is, God in the Image and Likeness made it so that practically, when you do some action, some at least one element should be, similar to you, a sort of young one. And for this, you have to select some single object in the perception system, it can be any object, for example: a voice recorder, a pen, or just some kind of material object.

And then you are going out to an object, for example, of an intangible type, suppose the primary thought of human, human as such, and this human is not personally you, but the primary thought of human when God created human. That is, we are all the time, all the time, standing at the origins of creation, in this case, of creation of human.

And when we for example finally ... Let's suppose, we have to heal a child, right?... and the child is young, and if to do some other control, and if the human is old, it turns out, we begin to perceive the difference in age in such a way that the effect of rejuvenation is, in fact, the action for another one, by the way. People cannot be cut off from this process. With your rejuvenation for a millisecond, other people, but to a lesser extent, should also rejuvenate in some way, that is, they should also have more health.

And therefore it turns out that the main primary level is any approached element where you have to see, as if to follow, the level of rejuvenation. Well, if there is some kind of pen, it might just like appeared a year ago, then you should move on to some other thing, standing nearby, and so on, but already standing at that time.

And in order not to look for different objects in the control system and not to lead them into this earlier time, you have to integrate the whole World so, that your Consciousness chooses independently, even in that level when you are not concentrating on this process, and you are naturally young. Well, the state of natural youth, right?... of natural health. After all, initially such level was expressed in human so. And that means that some external loads, external systems, which exist as an external control, actually should not, for example, lead to the exhaustion of cells, they should be, in general, a system of favorable action for human.

That is, a purely technological task arises: to transfer any level of control into the structure of a favorable action. That is, even if the level is some kind of stressful or unfavorable, then a favorable value is taken from this spectrum, and it is transfer into the structure of health of the person. How, in general, to pick out the desired value from an unfavorable spectrum? It is very easy, by the way. It is enough to review some future structural events or simply look into the future.

Actually it is very easy to look at the future from this position. When you initially know the point of creation of a human, and you are in it, and you are approaching, for example, according to this lecture, according to this methodology, and you just concentrate on the future for a while, literally the primary impulse – and, after a millisecond, this is the future. It is often not necessary actually to define positions first, it is enough to fixate the desire that the future should be positive. That is, the very pictures can be viewed later; in this methodology, we have to work, in general, quickly, because youth – is a quick phenomenon, right?

And when we begin, suppose, to draw the structure of health, then we just need the impulse of the norm, which we have, that is, we want norm, and at the same time we see it from the future, we understand this signal, then this level of signal passing through some unfavorable possible event is actually the platform for this event. So let's say the event comes in contact with the positive signal from the future, that is, the next event, well, it is some kind of link structure, the next link is positive, and we build it ourselves. Well, we do so in any control, we set some tasks and solve them.

And when we, in this level of a certain unfavorable event, outline the spectrum of a future positive value, then in fact we can scoop a positive status in any unfavorable event. That is, a human can be fully realized in any system, and at the same time live quite favorably, even if the spectrum is unfavorable. This is an important characteristic for today's control, because in the conditions exactly of the technology of eternal life and eternal development, when global destruction of civilization is possible, of course, a human should strive to realize, to immediately turn into reality the eternal development, it must be concrete, that is, it must actually be executable now. This is so. And then he should, the person should master real systems of development under real conditions. For example, he treats some kind of disease, or if he is healthy, then he produces some kind of control actions right?.., and when you see the disease itself as an unfavorable system, and the detection of the positive status is the healing, right?... this is the technology of the next action.

That is, we have come to the fact that there is always a level of creating of exactly a favorable level from an unfavorable one. That is, the starting point of an action is exactly such an action that this sort of an unnecessary for us system, it is not always unfavorable, maybe we just don't need it at this moment, well, some information that is not used, right?... Then we can make some capture, that is, transfer this information to a future system, where it already exists, this reservoir, as it were, right?.. this volume, it looks usually just like a kind of informative glow, well, just like the light of the silver level, and then you transfer following yourself this, as it were, a neighboring area of Light in fact. And then you get used to it, right?.. after some time, and you begin to understand that you can carry along with you this little piece, like a kind of backpack all the time. So you get used to it and start to carry out control in such a way that this effect of the presence of youth, is as if the relic glow, the primary one, it is always near you from the beginning.

And when you begin to bring this structure along with you, actually consciously, giving to the functions of the mind, of action and, as it were, of the integration near you, and you realize that here you really are becoming a younger person at this moment, that's the transition from this state to a younger state. And the transition itself is finally a recovery. It is clear that the transition to a younger state is a level of greater health. But it may be that a person had some diseases at an earlier age, it turns out that he should not get – if to consider as a system of cells - into this kind of cellular system that is modified, but get into the younger state, but from the point of view of the norm. Here, by the way, the technology requires clarification. The rejuvenation should be such that you are healthy of course at an earlier age, even more healthy.

And it turns out that here you need to have a kind of closed control loop, some kind of eight, that is, there is the following age, you withdraw from it everything the most favorable for the current time and transfer to the young state with all your luggage, right?.. with all the experience that you have now. It turns out that you are not just young, you look younger, logically you have larger experience, more ability to cope with the situation, and you additionally really transfer the cellular system to a new level, that is, you are even healthier.

And it turns out that here, if we think how God in general arranged the system of His own eternal life, of self-recovery, or of eternal development, then in fact it turns out that God every time becomes younger. And if He, for example, at the level of cell information, but in order for Him to retain the form of an ordinary human, He has to create some kind of static, well, how to say, exactly the static body system, for example, right? .. like all people.

It turns out that the static system of the human body is an increasing development in the direction of greater knowledge and in fact greater youth, for example, of God. And, in general, really, when there is more knowledge, then a person can do more, generally speaking, right? .. to realize more of some systems. Then there is a certain paradox. God, for example, increases the speed of rejuvenation with each next level of the further development from the perspective of the logic of human, and He comes to the point of His level of creation at ultra-high speed, that is, he passes this point of self-creation at a super-high speed and gets into the structure which is behind it, that is, he is always in the system of control over Himself. The more He is rejuvenated, the more he accelerates the speed of rejuvenation. This procedure is quite understandable. Those who begins to engage in rejuvenation, can see that the speed is really felt, how it is increasing. The only issue is that people have a moral criterion, maybe they think how they will look for others – but now this is another issue. If a person has solved for himself the psychological aspects of rejuvenation, that is, he is ready to be younger and this fact does not confuse him, then, generally, this technology can be quickly realized, exactly where you begin to consider the structure of recovery.

There is a single criterion that at some time a person should somehow look as of specially appropriate age and carry out some social functions. And if you overcome these structures of Collective Consciousness, then the rejuvenation system, will be quite accessible to you in this technology. The main thing here is to see the transition point when God transitions to the point of His self-consciousness, that is, he is brought there at high speed, right?.. if we can say figuratively, into the structure of self-control, and moreover, He is there in His Physical Body. Then it turns out that, yes, the body is really eternal, it is always in the system of control over its own events.

Then, for example, it turns out that any thought is an action; any structure of action - is some kind of already implemented action, a desire is new healthy cell, and so on. Let's assume that a human is always healthy, then the issue will be more about the control over events, because, as a rule, the level of health should be normalized in the control. And in this regard, it turns out that if, suppose, we have a structure of complete health, then it is the level of entering the control over events.

And in order to have more favorable events, more favorable level from the perspective of God, when there is a thread of this eternal development and this thread is unwinding, that is everyone can live within this terms, right?.., they exactly can developed eternally. Why, for example, cultural values, where there is a transfer of knowledge, experience, are always protected by the state and by people, and there is a level of spiritual knowledge here. The Spirit transfers primary knowledge, and so on. That is, the spiritual level is initially eternal, and the Spirit is working in terms of the transfer of knowledge or some information, but if, for example, we do the same for the physical body by control, well, you should just make a mechanical replacement.

There is a history of the development of civilization, some kind of cultural and moral values; moral values are understandable enough, for example: just some works of art, some values of cultural aspect – and all of this is some information. We, for the control with the human body, just as a model level, insert the body into the cultural layer, into this glow, that is we put the body outside the system of primary implementations of these actions, well, for example, some kind of folk art or some kind of historical religion, maybe original orthodox, and we see how the interaction with this information of a human, of the physical body of a human occurs. That is, the human is out of the system as if of the previous actions of people. And the human will live like that in the current time. This human, for example, when some kind of time passes, in general. The next time is still like a control over all that happened as it is considered in the past, right? ... From the point of view of God, it is a control over the future.

And when we understand how God, at the level of just logic, has already a level of control over the past and over the future, we can see here that the primary thought after creation was actually implemented, created in the same way by human himself.

And then we begin to understand this, that it is the thought, which is connected to him so close like the next world, right?... which is controllable by this thought, then we come into a very technological control system, where, practically irrespective of any region, it does not matter for the person where the horizon is, where the optical system is, where some method of control is, he can solve the system of control by a favorable level only because he is alive, healthy, or he is getting healthy, or he just carries out a positional control like God does. That is, he is doing the control, for example, from the point of view of the task. That is, if this is recovery – let it be recovery, if this is rejuvenation – ok, let it be rejuvenation, where there is a recovery, and so on. That is, if the system of action is specific, then there is a specific expression; if this is an event structure, then, it turns out, there still exists a system of certain, as it were, correlations.

That is, there is some kind of event and you have to control the event. You are engaged in rejuvenation. The structure of the primary action. At this second, I have done a control over some events, for example, control over the events of the audience or of the civilization, just, for example, of some certain events, and I get here the level that I need, that, for example each human was able to do a similar, for example, action through macro-salvation of all people, and he has a right to do whatever he wants: he may or may not do, or he may, for example, only be trained in this process, right?... and maybe he already knows this, because he himself is enlightened and has, or he just knows, as it were, from nature, he has it from God.

And when we have a lot of systems of control, this is exactly the kind of correlation level is the level when you begin to fix the primary control status from here. And when you work in the future environment, it turns out that you should be there the same person, who is located here now. And when you start to rejuvenate, what the main task is, by the way, what the subject of old age is, let's say, that is increasing information, that just increases the density of the control, and due to this the cells are loaded. And due to the fact that a human keeps the static now, in order to carry out a control into the future, his cells are beginning to deform, as if due to the light-optical tension.

And when you rejuvenate, in order to carry out a control, you have to highlight the status of the primary impulse. For example, like God does, He does the control initially, but with Him it's always clear that this is exactly the same God, the One. It turns out that, on the basis of this, you can also, in the same way, do some sort of correlation of the next level. That is, when you bring the control to a certain level, and when you rejuvenate, you have to correlate this Light with the current state. That is, you choose some intermediate position, for example, a position, somewhere as if from the side, you look at yourself from this position, look at all these exchange processes.

Well, you have a task, for example, you need to go to the store, buy something, no matter what. You just know that you will go there and will buy something, this is some action. It turns out that when you deduce this action that is in the form of a purchase, well, for example, it turns out, that you start to do it in such a way as if deducing this controlling impulse, well, as if drawing attention to the future segment. And it turns out that when you begin to draw attention to this future segment of external reality, to draw to this segment, which exists somewhere in the form of some kind of acceptor point of control, you begin to build, around you, as it were, some images that exactly attract attention, that is, you begin to transfer more information to yourself, that is, to increase the structure of age in practice. That is, you can be here at a younger level, or do exactly the healing procedure, and the structure of control of those processes which are there, they are such that concentration is taking place due to attracting some kind of attention to yourself, right? ... More attention - it means that it turns out that the array of chronological information is bigger at this point.

And when you begin to transfer here the structure of a control of this type, as the array of information that is there, it is bigger, you even the age, if you come to some primary age, let's say where, regardless of control, there is some kind of, let's say, single primary age, if we can say so, right? .. that is, as if a single age that allows you to control as much as possible, that is, the age approached to the action of God in this level.

And the question arises, for example, what the age of God is here. If you attract a lot of attention to yourself at this point, the more you attract attention, the more you take yourself to the level of control, that is, as if you are showing yourself, and the collective opinion is already formed on you, then you get, as it were, more control for yourself. But, in fact, anyway, any human who does not even attract attention, he still receives the same level of control from God. That is, everyone has the same structure of information transfer.

And it turns out that, based on this, there is a concept of the age of God in this action, precisely in action. That is, if we assume that the age of God is an infinite value, then how can we identify the age here, so that it would be clear how to compare with a human, for example? The easiest level of the human plan is to go over to the structure of awareness of personal infinite age and pick out one's own age on this axis. That is, for example, to assume that a human who was originally created, has an infinite amount of life, and then we just need to determine the coordinate at this moment, for example.

Well, here is the usual task of control: we just see in this namely time interval what is your age. That's when you take the structure of age under control from the point of view of the original endless process, where you are at once as healthy as possible, or completely healthy at the initial creation, it turns out that here we actually have such a level of control, that if we, for example, let's say, have made the control for information transfer, then have made some movement, aimed, suppose, at moving some simple thing, that is, we have made some movement near us, for example, or, we have made some kind of movement with our hand, then we have modified the information. And this modification has instantly accumulated the fact that some changes also begin to occur in the whole external environment, and what is more, they can be as if chaotic. So you did some, for example, purposeful action, moved something, and some structures of action take place in the external system related to this system, and they begin to look as if some kind of influence of the external environment. That is, the logical action transfers to the fact that some kind of unexpected actions are taking place in the external world.

But the world is exactly arranged this way. Some of your logical actions are necessary for you - and you meet the diverse world. That is why, in principle ... The world is arranged so, because actually the correspondence to the age of God is taking place at this moment, when you consider the line of your action, and how your event affects reality, you can see the structure of the age of God, for example.

And by the way, the action of the age of God can be seen in the internal structure of human. For example, in order to improve the health of a human, that is, in general, how can we determine that some organ of a human, for example, is unhealthy, or needs to be brought back to norm by the control? ... It is best to determine before he began to fall ill, that is, to go to the point where there is no disease yet, but there are some forecasting systems.

And the discrepancy between age systems, temporal systems, that is, the age of God at this moment, that is, the ideal level - God decided to do the same by Himself, then what age should He have at this moment, from the point of view of your physical birth? Then you immediately see what you need to do in relation to the organ. And this action, by the way, is infinite, that is, it is possible to bring this impulse at any distance and recover the organ. And that human will not even feel, he will just get it, that is, just the norm, and that's all. He will not perceive that there may have been some kind of, or could have been, a disease, and in principle, that the most natural, he will eventually understand that he did it himself, because he saw the action of God.

When he understands this, he already understands that, yes, it is possible. He begins to see the preceding picture that, yes, it is possible, there could be some kind of problem, but he correctly looked at God and received a concrete action, he had already received, as a matter of fact, an element of eternal life, that is, eternal life itself in his perception. As soon as he realizes this, he sees that any of his perceptions constantly carries this kind of eternal life thread. That is, it turns out that you constantly see the structure of control in such a way that, in any element of reality, in a sort of distant harmony of action, let's say, a human looks at reality, he has some problems, but whether the problems are, or not, there is a concept of deep harmony.

For example, in adolescence, a human enters the level when this level of harmony exists in the form of any action. That is, any action takes place, nevertheless, a human believes that this inner harmony, some kind of cricket of harmony, a cricket somewhere far away, it is hidden somewhere, but it makes a harmonious sound, that is, for example, we do not like it physically, but we like the harmony which is behind it, for example this harmony is silence. That is, some kind of inner harmonious meaning.

When you start to see the action of God towards you in this sense, it helps a person on the battlefield, for example, to survive in conditions where there are shrapnel. Well, during the Second World War there were many cases when ... or during fighting, that was exactly the level of internal harmony that actually saved a person, that is, the level of complete freedom. He can do whatever he wants at any time. That is, his inner action is completely free, he feels free: he did exactly what he wanted at that moment. It is the concentration on harmony, on the natural value that leads one to the fact that a human practically receives the structure of life along the line of freedom, originally given by God, that human should always live. And when he does everything he wants, he gets exactly the norm, that is, he lives in peace, for example, there are no shrapnel, and so on. And it turns out that we still have the task of real eternal development, because we are talking about eternal development, which means we have to talk about real categories, quantities, actions, technologies, and so on.

And in connection with this, it turns out that due to the fact that we have to do this really, we should, of course, get eternal development, rejuvenation, or recovery in any combination of events. And in this connection, of course, the task after all is special. Any combination of events is, after all, a certain structure of control associated with the fact that a certain wave often of many events is coming, and it turns out, that this layering of different waves is such that human should constantly draw some specific spectrum of specific personal private events.

For example, God is a personality. He gives Himself personal - for Himself He gives personal development to Himself as well. And the choice of the personal plan is a sort of private task of human. But when He sees that it is necessary to do the structure exactly of macro-salvation in action, it turns out that we already have such a level, that it is macro-salvation, that is, care for everyone, for every human, the action for all – this is actually a completely individual private task. That is, it turns out that he, this human, practically sees that he is revealed for God from the point of view of God, for example, in eternal development, in eternal youth and in eternal health in such a way that when he is doing for all, this is the level, as it were, of his personal, perhaps, way, which, although is private, but it turns out that it is precisely the action that is actually even for the whole World, it is a creative action, a certain lighthouse, a certain criterion, beyond which these values already are: here is eternal youth, for example, eternal life.

The fact is that the concept of eternal life implies any process. A person may have some old age, may then rejuvenate, maybe, let's just suppose, be young, but it turns to be that it is somewhat unnatural, but nevertheless, a human chooses a control structure as he wants, and, as a rule, the process is correspondence to age, then rejuvenation, correspondence to age, and so on, that is, as if amplitude-like.

And when you begin to consider such a periodic process as a structure, suppose, of the following action, it turns out that we see ... Well, for example, let's consider some light wave, any wave. There is a light in relation to the Earth, then it turns out that based on the fact that there is a reflection of some part of the light in the direction of the Moon, space and so on, we see a certain system of periodic actions. That's when, we in this state of a certain rest, decided to watch on a certain photon, and see how it develops in the structure of people in general, how it touches the tissue of people, right?.. Here I showed the light, how it touches the tissue. Some kind of light, in general, any, in outer space, how the interaction of one part of the light takes place, well, of some chaotic part.

As soon as we begin to set this task, we begin to understand its structure of development, then we see that God is initially very harmonious in respect to us, that is, He reveals some problems, in fact, in our situations. Well. Why do we need problems at all? It turns out that, logically, God simply could create a generally trouble-free structure of the World. And it turns out that, then there would be the linear principle of development, it does not give personal ... freedom to human. It is precisely from the point of view of freedom arises the necessity of such an action of God, that at some moment He begins to do some actions for us, such as identifying problems, right?.. His approach is the identification of problems. When God already acts Himself personally and begins to show what to do, for example, specifically, and the human begins to see His approach, the harmony arises from the search system. Well, this very photon of light. Why was human needed? For example, if study this photon. But what for? It was possible to do something else, but we wanted to study in such a way that it would result in eternal development.

And when we start to examine any phenomenon, from this position, it turns out that then there is no end, of course, of the study. We can do anything, and at the same time any processes that exist in society, generally among people, they are renewable, that is, there is no concept of an initial type of action. The event can always be brought to the primary most stable norm.

This, by the way, is a very powerful legislative level. Be very careful here, because what I have shown right now, well, actually pronounced, this situation is such that the most favorable moments in the life of human can always be restored in control. So, naturally, they can be expressed differently, not specifically, maybe for the same time, right?.. This is still the level of naturalness.

If your own Consciousness allows you to do it somehow in the Collective Consciousness, well it's ok, but to a greater degree it is the restoration of any most good condition for a human, which he considers necessary, right?.. From this point of view, the processes, for example, the process of universal resurrection, is just a general norm, and it turns out that it is the only one.

And when we, for example, proceed from this level, but, in general, I just showed it on the analysis of a certain photon, which has a periodic reflection. That is, a static element of light, which is somehow reflected in a dynamic form, connected some element of the form with an action, right? ... and realized that everything can be restored to the most favorable norm, moreover from a neutral level of analysis. Well some photon. What can be said about it, what he generally needs from the point of view of itself as a structure. It may not concern us at all, and nevertheless we draw such a conclusion.

Watch this action here, and you will see that in practice we can make a conclusion about infinity of our own development from any completely chaotic action of the external world. But when you get to yourself from here, that is, into your own Soul, or you begin to act with your own Soul, you will see that, generally speaking, your body is actually always healthy. That is, you have such a level that makes it possible to see it, in this case, in the form of such receptors of the body. That is, you see the future state of the body in a healthy form, when you already control, as it were, infinitely. Here you should always see that the lines of infinite control always come out from you, that is, everything is normal in infinity.

And here there is a level of specific local actions. Here you begin to understand clearly what needs to be done now. For example, if a person doesn't want to rejuvenate there, does he? Perhaps there is something specific, maybe it is due to some reason, if, suppose, he wants just to improve his health, or to cure someone, then this action is clearly traced as the only system of control in this technology.

By the way, what is very convenient in this technology is to find exactly what you need now. That is, to understand that, in principle, if we are doing such a control that, for example, we need to make a decision quickly, it turns out that, by the way, an interesting aspect of the choice of a solution in this technology is the structure of healing the body for an infinite time. That is, from infinite time, you understand that you are there, but, in some kind of an intermediate system, you can see, in principle, only what you need to do now in relation to yourself, for example, and in relation to other people. It is like a system of diagnostics, and a system of control aimed, for example, at eternal development.

And when, for example, you see the influence of some elements of the external world, it's like chaos, right?.. a certain structure of the external world, a certain structure, suppose of such control, that there is, suppose, some kind of comet, right?.. which can approach the earth, theoretically at least, a probabilistic value, and no matter which political or social systems, opinions of people are there, since there is the concept of an ordinary physical object. And we should be protected from these processes. And it turns out that this task of being protected from any processes, is the task of necessity of implementation, that we get optimal control for ourselves from any level, because we are actually helping this level.

And the transition, in fact, generally speaking, is very simple. When you work inside this particular system, which I have just told about, that you can bring any event to a favorable level, well, some of your earlier meetings that are in your memory, and so on. And when you start to see it already from the point of view of reality, you see that any current system is surmountable, when it is unfavorable or, if it is favorable, it can be improved. The space is a very mobile here. And you should observe, it is very well adjusted, it varies very well, and, in principle, in this space a human is always confident that everything will be favorable for him. He can enjoy nature, he can listen to music, he can be calm no matter what happens, for example, except for some, probably, incidents. I mean that it's like a background level, that there are no, of course, catastrophes, and so on. In case there are any problems, then, of course, he should concentrate and help to avoid primary manifestations in some specific problems, if this is a catastrophe. And I mean that, after all, in a usual state, human perceives the outside world often with tension, and it is the ability to find the norm at such a level this is also a special task for eternal development. Because often there are some events that are not noticeable for other people, they can burden or somehow act negatively, for example, on human health, and so on.

And in this connection, when we have, suppose, such a level of development that we overcome this state, perhaps periodically, not necessarily permanently.

Well, of course, all people are busy, but at least sometimes you should reach the level of harmony, as it were, in any case. For example, you have a lot of events that are very concentrated, often they are not necessarily bad perhaps, just a lot of things, and at some time you need to get to the level of such a deep macro harmony, of deepest harmony, where you see the action of God in relation to human, when He already created him, and at this He gives him the first knowledge this is a sort of quite a harmonious level. If we do not assume that if some kind of knowledge is large, then it turns out that there is some kind of load on the human. But, for example, we come to that it is not stressful for the human, he listens with pleasure to this knowledge of God. When we, for example, begin to look at this picture, visualize, enjoy nature, then, in this case, as if a systemic adaptation of human exactly to such favorable impulses of eternal development arises.

By the way, I introduce another new concept now, it is from eternal development, where there is the spectrum of a favorable level, and, in fact, all eternal development should consist exclusively of favorable levels – the farther, the more independent from any external systems, and human should develop more and more favorably. Generally speaking, this is also such a necessary task for solving some future issues. That is, each next level should be more favorable, more sustainable in fact. And this structure of finding the sustainability, often in difficult situations, this is something that a human has to do periodically, well, at least once every three years, well, roughly speaking, I am just self-analyzing, you can do it more often.

That is, it is always necessary to try to understand that you have achieved the next higher class of control and, in principle, it is better if you can evaluate it informatively, not even through logical systems, but by full control over the information. Here there is a sort of all information of the World. Though it is even more difficult in this situation, there are things that indicate that it is still much better. Learn to derive this structure of control and, by the way, you will see that here, by the way, an example of rejuvenation is a purely technical action in this level. Because then it turns out that, in this case, rejuvenation is generally a necessity.

That is, pay attention, I move on to the next level of more voluminous information, where rejuvenation is taking place as, in general, a necessary element which should be mastered by human as a mere technical element. And then you seem to get used to the idea that in order just to do some elementary actions from the point of view of eternal development, you should be able to rejuvenate at least if necessary, well, to heal yourself is considered as if self-explainable here. So, if you have time, it makes sense to devote time sometimes just for prophylaxis, well, as a rule, the main number of people rarely engage namely in prophylaxis, but nevertheless, if there are some primary signs, even informative ones, some problems start to occur, then you should give yourself at least a few seconds, it is often enough to ensure that you may not look at this information for a few months again. This is as a rule. It is typical, by the way, information for those who is involved in rescuing. And so if, of course, a person, for example, has already some problems and needs to solve them, then he should give himself more time, of course.

And then an element of permanent control of one's own tasks arises. And from the point of view, in general, if a human has brought himself, as it were, to the point that it is necessary to solve rather complicated problems, well, not necessary brought himself, may be the problems are difficult by themselves, it's just that his system has been realized in his life this way, let's say so, since human chooses his own life for himself and, as a rule, builds events for himself, that is, he seems to be face himself, right?.. in the structure of the eternal world. And it turns out that here he has to make some efforts, this is his personal task given him from the very beginning, from the creation. And, by the way you, can see there practically, in general, initially, what God actually put before human.

And if, for example, we have, some level of reality related to the fact that God has set, say, some specific tasks personally for a human, you can see how he listened to them: what He, God whispered to him, or how He initially told him, that it is the primary level of contact, how God generally told, was it a whisper in some intimate silence, or there was a sound, a rumble or something? You can watch exactly the conversation with God at this level of action, that is, the initial conversation of God, the initial one, of human and God.

And when you begin to enter such level, you see that any events that are around you have been overcome by you in terms of your personal action, when you are calm, confident, you are constantly doing something, that is, a normal condition of human as a rule. So you just bring the usual way of working to the level of the primary contact with God. That is, it is enough to see it once, and you will always see it. And then, it turns out, there is no break in your further actions, because you know your task.

Well, everything is very simple. A human, let's say, is a traveler, who knows the task, he knows it, but he is doing, he needs nothing in addition, he knows the task and he is doing it. Of course, some subtasks change somehow in the structure of control, but precisely the primary sense of the primary task is the main thing in this case. Generally, for eternal youth, it is often enough for a human actually to hear the primary task, or at least to see the place in the information, where it was set by God for you to be exactly stable, let's say, in eternal development. In order to live eternally you can just technologically apply the methods, and that's all. And I meant that if you live eternally, but as if without straining systemically, without being constantly engaged in control, without wasting time for any special control procedures, but just naturally live eternally, because human is like that by himself.

Then it turns out that here the control should be applied up to the moment when you have found some root system, some sort of essence, and then the next control is underway already. Well, in general, the methods are often just created for you to understand something in terms of the fundamentally new processes of building the World. And it turns out that when you, for example, understand this, you have completely different tasks. Why do you need the same tasks? It happens that it is not necessary to have this level of tasks, that if we, for example, have done something, why should we repeat, right?.. life is constantly changing. The main thing for us is to find this inner contact with God, where you see that God is young, for example, He gave you information initially at the time of birth or before birth, and you constantly see this contact at this level. By the way, the contact can occur in childhood, not necessarily this happens when people are of older age, when a person is already an adult, it is just like the next level of this primary contact. And the main thing is to see this single point. And this connection exactly with God is the most powerful level of control, which gives both youth and health. When you start expanding it, you actually get absolute control, and all your affairs are being implemented.

With this I finish today's seminar.

Thank you very much for your attention.

III
THE TEACHINGS OF GRIGORI GRABOVOI
ABOUT GOD
REJUVENATION IN ETERNAL LIFE

12 August 2015

Hello.

The topic of the lecture is my Teachings "About God". Rejuvenation in eternal life.

The lecture is held on August 12, 2015 from nineteen hours and sixteen minutes.

The text of the lecture is being created for the first time during its holding, which speeds up learning. During the lecture, the method of controlling forecasting to ensure eternal life is used.

Rejuvenation, which is characterized by body regeneration processes, restoration of certain spiritual characteristics corresponding to youth, as well as a certain level of the Soul development, which is characteristic of young years, all these components are directed, in eternal life, to achieve a certain wheel of information, where the primary point closes the starting point. And one should thus be able to change the structure of time in order to get the rejuvenation that you want at the level of the Soul. That is, here, with the technologies of eternal life, one needs to approach the structure of rejuvenation very finely, not as to any temporal aspect of just youth for a certain period, but as to a mechanism that ensures eternal life. And at the same time, the characteristic of infinite time, which manifests itself as a completely unambiguous characteristic of exactly the life of the organism, is, in this case, realized in the form of specific technologies.

And here it should be taken into account that that level of time return also characterizes the possibility of returning not only the temporal interval, but also a certain level of events that characterizes the person. And at the same time, for example, he would like to accomplish these events in his youth and accomplish some of his personal levels of implementation. Therefore, the complex structure of rejuvenation that exists in the positions of eternal life characterizes actually the fact that when you look, for example, at distant information of the future, you see a certain level of reaction of some external information objects.

Well, we can assume that you are looking at a tree in the future. And here, a specific technology immediately arises: the signal coming from the tree rejuvenates you, but in such a way that you realize everything that I have said in this lecture, that is, you realize your own true personal tasks as well. Therefore, approaching the structure of rejuvenation, it is necessary first of all to consider what specific personal tasks you solve in your any actions, in your realizations, in professional, for example, activity or in other areas of activity.

And here it is important to note that it is namely the concept of personality tasks, that is, the characteristic that forms, first of all, the future events, so you can clearly plan, for example, some events of the current time as well as of the past, so that the characteristic of rejuvenation itself covered all periods of time, including also past time.

And here, in the technologies of eternal life, just lies the main essence of the technology of rejuvenation, that all events are unified to the level of the current moment. And while any element of time in the past practically is not differentiated as, for example, a separate element, since it is an integral part of some multitude of information in the future.

Thus, we can consider a very interesting characteristic of rejuvenation, where elements of the past are used as some kind of matrix systems for any future rejuvenating events. At the level of logic this is a memory of some good moments, for example, these are any elements that you remember as the fact that you would like to achieve this specific goal. And even after reaching the goal, it is advisable, with the rejuvenation mechanism namely in eternal life, to return to the brightest, most impressive moments in the past, where you would like to be realized or achieve something concrete.

Then it turns out that this matrix function, which bases namely the rejuvenation structure as the whole spectrum of future events, is formed due to favorable events of the past. That is, in the structure of rejuvenation in eternal life, there is such an interesting phenomenon of control as a look into the past, which has a very good series of events. Thus, we can very quickly, if we imagine on the physical level, as if to turn around sharply and see the future; and the feeling that remains of a good past, of good events of the past can be sharply transferred to the future.

And here is the technique of rejuvenation, it is caused precisely by the fact that when you are informationally and physically on the platform of eternal life in terms of the information development of external information, then when you make such a sharp movement with a look into the future, then the light from the good events of the past that stopped as if in your view, on your body or managed to reach it, at this moment is sharply transferred to the future. Thus, you, as a matter of fact, as if weave a certain fabric of the future, you create the matter of the future due to, in general, previous events or initiatives already created in many respects.

And here comes just the same radical moment in terms of control systems for rejuvenation in eternal life, that is you need to build completely new events that you will need. But, as a rule, a person, in the process of development, often absorbs certain rather long long-term structures. For example, a person can love eternal time, and at the same time he must ensure a certain level of stability of a particular development that ensures this love for infinite time. You can also refer this to your own body.

The Creator who created eternal life, first of all considered himself as the realizer in all aspects of this eternal life, and therefore, in this case, we can also say with confidence that when implemented in all systems of eternal life, you get exactly the fullness of youth in eternal life. At the same time, it is necessary to take into account that this fullness itself is determined by your criterion for the onset of rejuvenation, because some quite curious individuals, for example, can delay the beginning of the rejuvenating process in order to know some elements of aging or, for example, age characteristics of external social environment. At the same time, they, for example, heard from grandfathers, grandmothers a lot of some stories, they saw some events that were conducted by grandfathers and grandmothers, by parents and young people, and, in this case, some people have a certain element of cognition or the need to know this state of a certain old age level.

In this regard, we must proceed from the fact that, since this, in general, is a good characteristic - everyone has the right to a certain level of aging - nevertheless, it should be taken into account that, it is desirable to insert into each period of aging the information of youth that as if exists covertly, for example, intracellularly, in the process of aging in the conditions of eternal life, like some powerful potential energy, if we compare it with some kind of waterfall that is somewhere behind the dam: as soon as the locks are opened, this waterfall descends abruptly.

What is it for? The fact is that during the aging process, some functions of the organism can either be slowed down or modified in the direction that needs to be adjusted, and therefore, just in case, you need to reserve a certain element of youth as if in the aging process. This mechanism is as follows. You imagine any of your cells, just one. Then, due to the right hemisphere of the brain, you bring this information out to the comprehension that this cell is such that the whole organism is structured the same way. And you enter as if a duplicate or, so to speak, a copy of this cell in a reduced size under the upper surface of the cell, and this copy, in some cases, is in contact with the borders of the real cell from the inside.

Thus, you can consider the mechanism of how youth exists inside an aging organism and at the same time you can initiate, so to speak, old age that is growing younger, in fact, if, in this case, we can introduce such a concept, for example. And then you can consider the development of cellular systems in the way that happens in a child. That is, the more you move, for example, in terms of aging, the more your body, in this technology, should perceive precisely the development of cellular systems in the child. In this case, first of all, you need to imagine yourself in childhood, but you can, for example, consider everything that is young from the point of view of logic, for example, there is a young plant, animal, young world in some kind of civilization, and so on.

And when you consider the process of this youth, very powerful, in general, such huge prospects open up before you, related to the fact that you combine aging, for example, if you want, and youth at the same time.
But there is a category of people who want to exclusively preserve youth for a sufficiently long visual, or, generally speaking, eternal, for example, time. Then, for this category, first of all, it is necessary to synchronize

one's thinking with the fact that there are people around who, for example, want to get old, some want to be even younger and not get old. Then the question arises, again, of unification in the general development of civilization and of some general systemic approaches in choosing a certain path in the development of civilization as a whole, of humanity, for example, or any living creatures there. Then it turns out that these same ones, for example, if living beings live on planet Earth simultaneously with humanity, it turns out that we have a certain phase of collective Consciousness, where the aging process is laid out in a certain logical form.

Now, if you think about it, then you can consider such a fairly obvious point that many social processes are practically arranged so that the aging of a person is taken into account, for example, reaching retirement age, payment of pension funds, and so on. That is, a certain template, according to which a person should be guided, as it were, and he is offered a certain structure of his future processes, possible, in cases where he follows the levels of aging.

It is important here to lay some areas, namely of eventful, informational youth, into the social processes that occur in life. That is, regardless of age, for example, to work, to be active, cheerful, to consider events positively. And in the event that some unfavorable event rolls over, it is necessary to try, at the level of the hard impulse of the Spirit, when you feel the absolute stiffness of the Spirit, in this regard, that it is focused on eternal life, you should always feel this state at the level of, for example, heart, at the level of the spine, even purely physically, that nothing will change your structure of eternal life.

Here, the concept of exactly of an unfavorable event is just such that even if, at some moment, a person thinks what to do, for example, how to transform the situation for the better, in order to overcome old age and to ensure that the attainability of eternal life was objectively constant, this core here enables you to base on your specific experience. That is, it is important here: why is it preferable to practice a lot in control, for example, according to my Teachings in the field of rejuvenation, in the area of eternal life? Then a certain automatism arises, in which, even if you are distracted in thinking, do not hold this thought, you still remain on the spiritual, or as if at automated spiritual-bodily, soulful level, or even on the way of control, so to speak. And when you are considering here exactly such a trend of control related to the development and stability of spiritual abilities, it is important to note here that with the true motives, some true personal goals, which may be few at first, and when they say, for example, to a person "the whole life is ahead," he feels some enormous prospects. And, for example, in this case, for the eternally-living one, it is always like this: all life is always ahead. And it turns out that when we say this, at the level of information, this is one thing, but when we say at the level of logic, at the level of understanding the physical, spiritual, and informational processes of eternity, we can see that life, namely physical, (the spiritual life in eternal life as well, to a certain extent) - it seems to be coiling like a spiral. That is, if you pay attention to how a person begins to perceive himself, it will look like a big circle, that a person has physically walked around some kind of, for example, a big circle, a circular area and approaches himself, but in an earlier age.

Here it is necessary to pay attention that exactly this approaching has the characteristics of impulses. That is, at first a certain impulse is coming, you begin to see some events that may have surrounded you in childhood, but which you did not pay attention to. Then you can get closer to yourself in information and at the level of thinking, but here there is a very serious interweaving of thinking and physical reality. And if you recall some moments in childhood, well, maybe somewhere around 12 years old, somewhere around this interval, most likely, this is largely determined by the individual characteristics of the person, but there may be some additional contacts somewhere up to 14 years, perhaps. And you can see that if, for example, you want to contact yourself, for example, at the age of 21, in this case you are doing it at the level of the current conscious control, and not at the level, for example, of the natural law of the development of eternal life, which is as if driving even if you don't examine this technology at the level of controlling systems of personality, Consciousness, the Spirit and the Soul.

It makes sense here to consider such a process, well, as a certain story, that you approach yourself and enter into a certain telepathic contact. Remembering, for example, such a story, we can then draw a conclusion about eternal life, generally speaking, on the whole, because a contact with oneself in the future means the presence of a complete sort of a wheel, of a control cycle; and returning to any of the intermediate points means exactly the clear factor of eternal life. And, in this case, you can consider completely unambiguously such a moment that when you look at yourself from the side of, say, an adult person, an adult state, you see yourself at the same time and feel yourself young at the same time. But when you are in a state of action, you feel only young, looking at that one who, let's assume, is in telepathy, or, perhaps, who, to a certain extent, is even partially visualized, say, or somehow while standing apart, not at the level of direct view, is talking with you, and you can hear some rustling, if you do not want to approach at the level of some kind of partial visualization to yourself at an earlier age. And here a very serious moment arises connected with the interaction of this wheel of youth.

And here it turns out that at a certain moment, being at an earlier age, you instantly transmit some information to yourself. Here it is necessary to capture this moment and see what is transmitted. That is, maybe some objects that will be met in the future, maybe some images. And the most important is to see here for eternal life what information stream it is, that is, the style of this stream, its perception at the level of the Soul, at the spiritual level, how it is perceived by your Soul, that is, to grasp here the main essence as much as possible. And try to perceive, when you, for example, felt that such perception ended, try to perceive the capital letter "X", as if placed in front you. Then you can move this letter left, right. And we can see that if you turn this letter to the right, then information from the future comes to you, to the left - information from the past, but such that it is as if mixed with the future. And if you twirl this letter away from you along its axis at the intersection of the two segments that form this letter, it turns out that you bring the future closer, when you twirl to yourself, you move the future away from you.

And having learned in this way, for example, to work with such a symbol as the letter "X", that is, if in the Cyrillic alphabet it is the letter "x", it turns out that you can, generally speaking, work with other letters in the same way. For example, this letter sounds as "X-a," that is, "ha", then we can work with the letter "a". Well, not exactly the same, of course. We can, in order to understand how to work with the letter "a", imagine that it consists of many letters "X". And then it turns out that you begin to feel the mechanism of work with the letter "a". Thus written works appear in eternal life in terms of connecting the infinite future with the infinite past.

And here the question arises precisely about your infinite past. Since there is a certain date of birth, in order to prolong your information to the preliminary previous infinity, you can just go out to this infinity from the date of birth by volitional effort and develop your personality by means of Consciousness, by some informational energy ray just to the infinity that was before your birth. Technologically it looks as follows: you imagine, at the nape level, a ray coming from you, and at the same time it goes, so to speak, to minus infinity, where there are some events, and you just keep it with an effort of consciousness.

But here we should bear in mind a very interesting paradoxical system of space in eternal life. Since the past and the future intersect there, you can fall into certain intervals of the future in some sections. And here these elements of intersection, which I spoke about, the meeting with yourself in the past, often happens regularly and it can be so frequent that you can see yourself at minus infinity, that is, at the heart of the organization of the world.

Then it turns out that since the world was simultaneously created in one impulse, everything was created actually simultaneously. That is, if you look at the frame, for example, of a spray of water in slow motion, you can see that everything is as if developing slowly, and every drop, if it were somewhere before, is slowly spreading in some place or is scattering. And now here, if we go to the slowed down picture of the development of the primary impulse of the world, we can see that the Creator defined certain specific places for everyone in the level of development at the time of the emergence of the world, and for every system of reality in general. And, having found yourself there, you can clearly say that having such a position, already stable, because you have found yourself by Consciousness there, in this case, the conversation with God that takes place at your level of the deep foundations of the Soul is actually forming not only your body in the future, and in the infinite future, but is also forming your Soul.

That is, through verbal conversation with God, you can form your own Soul, which, it would seem, as the eternal structure originally created, to be little susceptible to any change in terms of the processes of eternity, but it turned out that in this case, inside eternity, the structure of the Soul can be formed. And so, an initially soulful person, having the Soul, with developed spiritual abilities, begins to choose for himself, some such a suit or some clothes in the level of his initial minus infinity of his development, in the starting point of the world, in order to put it on the surface of the Soul.

And here it is important to see that the Spirit was originally still highly developed. And when you put on certain clothes, you begin to act within these clothes. And maybe it is embarrassing somewhere, maybe it gives some new creative possibilities, but this clothes is clothes, the clothes of the Soul or spiritual clothes, and it realizes the hope of certain events that should develop in the future. So, there should be not just the hope for events, but there should be concrete clear events that were initially formulated, maybe just in your idea, in terms of what you want from life, how you want to organize it. And this idea holds the whole future like a kind of peculiar cone. That is, the ray coming from you, it implements everything in this, or everything is realized on it.

And it turns out that, in this case, we can definitely and absolutely say that when you look at the future in this way, you see that, generally speaking, you organize the whole future on your own, with the participation of the Creator, of course, and with the help of many people who help you and surround you. Nevertheless, the basic level of your inner impulse, the main essence of your idea, for example, your eternal love, your goals that you must achieve, all this moves the future and determines it.

And thus it is clear how the Creator created the world immediately. He created it on his own idea of eternal life and at the same time he gave this idea to everyone. And when all ideologists are in the same direction, then, further, everything can be done easily and simply, so to say. But here you need, of course, to detail, everyone needs to be trained in the same way as the Creator did, to spread his idea of eternal life into the infinite future, making a concrete effort to that.

Considering some processes taking place in the world, one can observe some events, in which there is the presence of the Creator. God is present in completely different events. And at the same time, we can see that exactly the orientation toward the area of eternal life is latently or explicitly happening everywhere: in any event, in any moment. And at the same time, we are quite able to see that when we, for example, realize the structures of eternal life into the structures of distant infinity, that is, what is brought closer and that is a perceived infinity, it would seem, somewhere close, and a person can master this infinity and calmly develop. But if generally to transfer to some distant worlds, that is, to move to the level of global thinking, and to consider the development of matter from the point of view of the Creator, it turns out that one eternal life, which, in this case, you have, and, for example, which you see in others, is such that you can see that it is necessary to unite in achieving eternal life by all, then all infinite spaces will be mastered. And rejuvenation in the conditions of eternal life implies and means that, generally speaking, all the spaces of the world should be mastered, although it is developing endlessly, but nevertheless such a goal exists and it will be realized. And this, by the way, is precisely a spatial, physical goal, which contributes to eternal life.

If you think about the question: why was space created? why, for example, God did not create a life form such that there was some kind of closed system, like, for example, when some mechanisms live somewhere in the ocean in the Mariana Trench, there is development and some microorganisms exist; and they have everything there in a closed level where there is no light, and they seem to autonomously exist in some kind of information. But the whole world is very diverse, and, as a whole, of course, it is not like that. But when the question is: why the world was created diverse, then here is just one of the answers, it is such that when a person, sets the task of achieving precisely the distant, that is, all infinity in eternal development, all infinity of the world, then a definite goal arises for him. That is, the goal set by God by creating space.

And, based on this, it turns out that you can define your youth, in the structure of eternal life, as that genetic system, which is the system of development as well, which reacts to the goal. That is, you should learn to perceive your genetic system - this is an infinite space - through the task of mastering this space. Since the genetic system in many ways looks closed, for example, if we recall a certain level of micro, micro-life, for example, micro-level in some ocean, we can say that life, around the genome of a person, is developing as rapidly as around this micro-system, for example.

Then it turns out that you can develop the gene fully preserving it in that material form as it is, but you can develop certain structures of the human gene that are close to the spiritual characteristics, and the gene, in fact, begins to develop independently. And when, for example, you fall into some space of the future, you already have a memory of this space in the genes. That is, you are laying it to yourself at the level of a natural, as is commonly believed, evolutionary development, when the previous experience in the development of living organisms seems to be focused on the genetic system, and it largely responds to a changing reality system taking into account this genetic experience. In this case, the technology includes the development of a similar mechanism that exists in the collective consciousness and which means that you will have a sustainable development in the future through the organization of your own genetic system.

Here, in order to organize it correctly in this context, you should first of all see yourself from the surface of the skin. For example, look at yourself in the infinite future from the point of view of the skin of the right arm, then the left one, the right hand, then the left hand, then the feet, and then examine yourself from all sides and see that if things, which are not needed, start to occur somewhere, that is, they affect somehow undesirably, for example, even the skin, that is, some kind of pressure occurs, then you should exclude these events, withdraw them from the level of events. And it looks, at the level of control like, for example, a walnut breaks, a click occurs, and it turns out that there are good grains inside, that is, good events.

When we consider the phenomena of the physical world, we see that if we proceed from the position that the world was created through wave systems, that is, a microsystem is also as a system with wave functions, we can see in this case that this sound transfers into action. That is, a wave that creates, for example, a walnut, creates a sound wave with a click. That is, there is a certain level of causality and effect in the event structure of control. And when you look at the control system in such a way that you want to trace the basis of any phenomenon in general, you can connect, - for example, as in this example with a nut - the wave of primacy with the fact that it was the shape of the nut that was created for good reason in general, the nut has grown so for a purpose that it can create such a sound.

Well, this would seem doesn't have any particular applied value, it's just some particular variant in this case, it would seem, at first glance in relation to the nut. But if you look closely at any other object in the world, for example, a plant, an animal, some kind of manifestation in the world, for example, let's say, there is an example that an apple falls on Newton's head, and he, as the legend says, comes to the idea of the presence of gravity and so on. That is, some phenomena somehow occur.

And this is why I say this in such a context, because when we evaluate events in general, it turns out that every event exists for a reason namely in terms of eternal life. For example, according to the law of development of eternal life, as it has been said in this lecture, everything already existed in the center of the event from the very beginning. And then it turns out that this click of a cracked nut actually characterizes such a position of control that this sound is present simultaneously at the beginning of the organization of all events. But at the same time, - for example, I talked about this option in this lecture - it turns out that when we comprehend this process, we practically come to that level of control in this case, that all the events are here and now. And it turns out, when we come to this, we comprehend youth in the reality in which it is.

And, proceeding from just such a principle of creating youth in eternal life, you can see that the very level of youth quite clearly arises somewhere, starting, for example, near your body; the primary wave begins closer to the heart, and then it begins to cover the organism, and you begin to feel the strength. This feeling of power, which is like a string, arises, and it begins to fill the body, and you begin to sense it. Well, as it happens, apples grow, and you can directly feel the energy that fills the apples. There is even such a term as "rejuvenating apples". This energy actually begins to embrace you, and you really begin to feel young, where all the functions of the body work for you just like in a young person. The main thing is to stay in this state for longer, that is, to realize it as much as possible, reproduce it, and try to make so that this state covers practically all spheres of life.

And so, having such a state, you are quite able to conclude that you can control such state, you can reach such state, that is, you can have eternal youth. It is enough to understand and have a conceptual apparatus that indicates that there is eternal youth in eternal life, it initially exists namely as a cycle, and that it's only a person's personal will, sends us, for example, the aging for a certain period, but with the need for rejuvenation.

Of course, there is such a moment that a person can grow old, maybe he likes it, and he can be in this state for a long time, supporting, for example, old age for some long time. There are no exceptions here, in this case, we are talking about the fact that everyone chooses what he likes: there is no system of restrictions.

And there is one more conclusion from the axioms of eternal youth: there should be no restrictions in the structure of the choice of namely of the age state. Well, let's put it this way, there must be complete freedom, firstly, and even in general. And, in this case, there should be a situation regarding the fact that, first of all, you can accept freedom as a state. It is not about the usual physical understanding of "freedom", it is namely freedom of a possibility to make the choice of action, the ability to act. And it arises when you constantly do something, and you get that you have to solve issues permanently. This is also one of the objective forms of your freedom, and it is expressed in your achievement of eternal life without fail, which means the achievement of some goals, and so on.

And here, at the level of freedom of action, such a moment arises that after all it is possible to achieve any goal in eternal life. And now, if the goal, which has already been achieved and realized by you, suddenly starts to change, because the goal has a certain form of events, if a certain series of events occur, if suddenly any events arise that are undesirable, and they need to be corrected, then you just need to return to the past and, as often as possible, correct it from the past. That is, as if aligning the entire layer of events from the level where you reached it, and you have this event at a good level, and right to the level where you would like to restore the structure of events. In this case, you should be able to think clearly in terms of the fact that you should practically try to perceive the structure of events in such a way that the event that happened and which is aligned, it should be aligned at the level of your goals, so as you implemented this event in such a way as to ensure that it was generally perfectly implemented.

And here it is necessary to find some kind of systems, because if a distortion of the achieved event occurred, some justification is needed - why this happened. As a rule, in eternal life - and generally speaking, this is the law - the situation always goes in the direction of improvement. And it turns out, if there is something here that you do not like radically at any period, try a bit to come up to an idea, that is, formalize the state. Try to think that you, as a person who realizes eternal life will still, after some time, come to a calm good level, or to a joyful level there, not necessarily calm, to some good level in your understanding. And at the same time, you will have to understand at that moment, that everything has already leveled off anyway in the future. That is, at the moment of any, for example, crisis situations, you should try to imagine at least mentally that, in the future, everything will still be according to the norm, since this is the law of eternal life.

And based on this, here is one more of the criteria for achieving eternal youth in eternal life or, for example, rejuvenating which is mandatory at all levels of development of eternal life, this is to try to draw a certain ray from oneself to a normal event and to know that this event will be. It would seem such an elementary action, but very effective from the point of view of methodology. You should just visualize somewhere around the level of the ribs, between the ribs, where the solar plexus is, you draw out the beam from there and at least remember that the norm is in any case ahead. And it turns out that you normalize in this way with a simple impulse, in fact, you normalize all reality.

So, comprehension of all the said processes of realization in eternal life, the realization of youth in eternal life is such that you can completely, based on some of these mechanisms and techniques, realize youth, eternal youth or youth in eternal life and at the same time teach all others.

Thank you for your attention. The lecture is over.

IV

THE TEACHINGS OF GRIGORI GRABOVOI ABOUT GOD.
THE METHODS OF REJUVENATION IN ETERNAL LIFE

October 12, 2015

Good afternoon.

The webinar topic is The Teachings of Grigori Grabovoi "About God". The Methods of Rejuvenation in Eternal Life.

I am going to consider a number of approaches to consider various methods of rejuvenation. First of all, we will consider the physical model which is the most prevalent in Collective Consciousness.

Thus, we said that first of all we will use the approach with application of the physical principle of the world structure. It is well known, that micro particles can be considered both as a micro-wave, and as a particle. And when considering the wave level of the structure of the world, we can consider the following process.

First, the method of rejuvenation with the use of the wave principle includes the allocation of the wavelength. While the whole organism is considered at the wave level. When we consider the atom as a wave, we can give the atomic level the required property through the resonance of another wave. In this case, the properties must be such that correspond to young organism. For this purpose, it is necessary to consider first the source that can create constantly such a resonance in eternal life. In this case, if we consider the source, which correlates with eternity, this is the thought of man. It is easy to see that human thought is created without using the material resources of the physical organism.

The Creator created the world using external information. Based on the same principle you should consider your thoughts that are the source through which the thought is created out of the resources of the organism. It is logically understandable, because the organism is examined, and the thought is external information. Therefore, through access to external information through our Consciousness we get the source to refuel the thought. This source is additionally defined through number series: **848741**. Thus, through this series we get immediately into the desired coordinate of a thought, from which we can send an intensified resonance wave to the right atom and the right molecule, respectively.

The whole organism can be described with the wave theory. Thus, to rejuvenate the body using the eternal source, it is necessary to send the light wave from the thoughts to certain coordinates of the atoms in the human body. A quantum video camera that can distinguish light of thinking was created in the Institute of Radioelectronics. If you direct the video camera towards man, the light of thought shows up in the area of the head.

When you use this number series, you should focus your attention in certain places near the head. And when we work with the resonance wave, you have to intensify it. To amplify the wave, which you take out from a thought and distribute to your atomic-molecular level, you should use concentrations on external objects. In the concentration on external objects, respectively, you should take into account that there is a certain level of cognition on the part of the human Soul.

When the Soul cognizes the world, it already has the knowledge and at the same time gets it from external information. When you use this approach, you can get information due to increase of speed. That is to say, the information from the external environment should enhance the wave so quickly as if it had already been inside the organism. In practice, it is approximately like that: when you quickly move your gaze, you simultaneously grasp two nearby sites.

Similarly, you can imagine fast action of the Spirit that moves the light from the external space inside the body. The Spirit is endless; therefore, it does it instantly. The information outside the organism and inside is equally the same for the property of the Spirit due to its infinity. The Creator also perceives everything in a single view, and therefore external infinite information gets into the organism.

* * *

There is information in my patents "The Information Carrying System" that, for example, says that the signal exists almost simultaneously both in the source, and in the receiver. The same principle is used, and the same method is used in the patent "Method of Prevention of Catastrophes and Device for its Realization". Therefore, when we intensify thus the wave that comes from the thought, we get a rejuvenation due to normalization of the wave, which corresponds to the atom: we intensify the wave that corresponds to a rejuvenation through the atom.

Hence, we can make a conclusion that the most important thing here is to distribute clearly, what we do at each level of control. The task, as it is clear, is to bring the wave from the thought into the atom, and the external radiation of the environment is used only as an amplification of this wave. For example, the device "Method of Prevention of Catastrophes and Device for its Realization" contains an amplifier in the form of small laser radiation, external radiation. The function of the patent is normalization of information in the field of control. In this case, man does the same kind of work due to his thinking.

The next task: it is necessary to determine the access points into your organism to get into the correct atoms, through which you will rejuvenate. To determine on the body the access points, you have to solve the task of achieving eternal life. That is you should look with the hidden spiritual vision at all your events in the infinity, at your life events, or of another person in respect of whom the work in the infinity is carried out. You should find in the spectrum of events the spectrum of infinity, that is, where life events do not stop. And see where the rays from this source, from this spectrum, fall on the organism.

Methodologically this is simple enough: at a distance of about three meters, you should see the point of this spectrum that generates rays toward your body or toward another person's body, or even toward all living people, if you specifically provide eternal life to another person, or everyone. These points, they are clearly felt. So to speak: clearly perceived points on the organism because the concentration is felt.

There is such a notion as "solar wind", which can move even physical objects in a vacuum. The feeling is such as if there is a pressure of the concentrated air on your skin. Some people feel it immediately as some stroking or some soft wave inside the organism in certain internal organs. This is the work of function of imagination of man. The imagination develops up to the level of connection of imagination with the real physical situation in the world.

This method contains a sub-method, which makes it possible to develop instantly the imagination of a person with a clear connection with reality, with the controlling reality. For example, when I diagnose aircrafts, I identify a defect that is in reality, or the norm of the technical condition of the aircraft. I can also imagine that the technical condition of the aircraft is normal, but in the information of control, the area of control is near the aircraft, and it is not connected with the aircraft. Thus, the sphere of imagination, by an effort of will, should be joined with the aircraft for accurate diagnostics.

And the essence of sub-method is that you have to join the wave, which corresponds to the youth, with the current wave that you want to transform into the wave that corresponds to a younger organism. Then you feel both the external rays, and at the same time, you work through your imagination. The external rays, they already contain the information of control toward rejuvenation, and you should further inform them due to your thinking. For this, you have to imagine yourself being younger: as far as you want. You can also use the method of self-diagnostics and exact level of energization of the wave for rejuvenation, for example of internal organs.

There are many methods how to inform your thought, among them there is a sub-method when imagination quickly transforms into controlling reality. To do this, you should determine, in the sphere of the thought, the sphere of imagination, and then determine the sphere of actual events. For those who have been doing control for a long time these spheres coincide at once, as a rule. Therefore, this level of informing the thought refers to those who has started working in the area of control. Those who have been doing control a long time, and these spheres are the same, have to solve the inverse problem, that is, to divide the spheres and to determine the sphere of control, as if withdrawing it back.

It is important to be able to do the job of the beginner level so that you could teach more affordably and quickly the person who begins to make control for the realization of eternal life. Since, educational

● ● ●

technologies are implemented in my Teachings, the components of the education, which enable you to train effectively, sometimes should be specially developed in this way, i.e., the process of control should be detailed. Having formed in this manner one of the options within your thought, you should carry with a mental effort the light from the area of thinking, which is mainly visualized in the area of the head; transfer it to the point of external environment, i.e. intensification of this thought. The point of the external environment, as I informed, is about three meters away from man and, as a rule, in front of the face slightly to the right toward the right shoulder. You should watch how from this point the thought of rejuvenation along the rays gets into those points of the organism, where you felt the concentration. I mean, this is what I said before, when external rays like the solar wind offer pressure on the skin tissue.

If we consider the property the usefulness of UV radiation on the skin and on the organism, it is possible in this case similarly to consider the usefulness of these rays of thinking and the external environment. View at the level of information the process of absorption by the organism, by skin of UV rays. And carry out the absorption of the rays in your thought with rejuvenation in exactly the same way, at the beginning.

It is simple enough to look at the level of information how the UV rays are absorbed: you have just to formulate the task and just observe how the processes of light exchange take place with such wording. The wording is that you want to see how the UV rays fall in their positive effect into the organism.

* * *

You will notice that there is an effect of a double wave: first, there is one wave, and the second one occurs simultaneously as if at this place and is absorbed immediately. You can consider such a process that ultraviolet rays are absorbed and give effect not through biological systems of the organism, but through the wave systems. To do this, you should look as though from the inside of the skin at how the rays fall on the skin, view the skin in the form of a wave and see how they get through the skin.

At the same time, you should explore with a hidden spiritual vision why they are beneficial to the organism, to which organs the wave or waves are distributed. If some of the areas are not very well defined or have a dark color, then you can use the sub-method, where imagination instantly becomes the control. When working inside the organism with wave the level this can occur very quickly.

While the sphere of real events is located in an area of the heart, somewhere within five centimeters from the skin outside of the body. And the sphere of imagination is located in the area of the right hemisphere of the brain approximately seven centimeters outside the skin. These spheres can be also identified by technical means, by an instrument control. Thus, from the area of right hemisphere, the sphere is quickly imposed on the sphere near the heart. So, you can quickly view the effect of ultraviolet rays, and on what organs and systems they have mainly the positive effect.

Unlike ultraviolet rays, the rays of your thought operate so that your organism lived forever. Having considered first the wave action of ultraviolet rays, you should imagine what would have happened if these actions had been eternal. And then you will be able to identify the points on the body that will be lighter when you view yourself or others. And thus you will be able to consider also the function of imagination, advanced towards infinity, and to determine in this process that these lighter spots on the human body roughly coincide with those points, which came from the outside and from the point of external environment that are within three meters from the body.

For example, when I provide number series for some controlling process, I in fact also set the coordinates of access of thinking to atomic, to the tissue level of man or to the environment. For example, in "The Numerical Atlas of Creation of Man and Eternal Life" I set the coordinate system of both the external and internal environment in relation to the organism, and at the same time the internal connections between these systems.

You have to identify the points of connection between the external rays that came out from the point, which was within three meters from you or from another person with whom you are working, which you revealed due to imagination that violet rays were endless, that is to say, they give infinite development. When you find these points you will see the physical form of the human body, you will also be able to view with your spiritual vision.

Applying the general principle, that the common more clearly gives the quotient, you will then accurately, strictly enough define the entry points of these rays into the skin of the body. I mean the "rays" from the point, which is three meters away from the body, and which (rays) carry exactly the information of the rejuvenation thought. Thereon the technology of this method is over. You get information of youth due to thinking, and thinking has the property of eternal obtaining information of energy of light. The thought does not use any tissues of the body and at the same time is an active level of the body. The right, built in such a way, structuring of thought makes it possible to rejuvenate the organism eternally.

The next method of rejuvenation in eternal life is that you apply the function of spiritual development to determine the functions of the rejuvenation of the Soul. For this purpose, it is necessary to develop the Consciousness to such a level that Consciousness includes the possibility of cognition of the rejuvenation of the Soul. The longer man lives, the more information he accumulates, therefore the Soul has more opportunity for rejuvenation. In infinite development, that is, in eternal life, this function is fixed; it is the state of the age of the Soul. That is, on the part of the Soul a work as if beyond the time is carried out, and basically control of event processes takes place. The Soul was created primarily in the structure of the world; therefore, it comes to its more natural state.

The method is to view your Soul through the spiritual vision, how the Soul rejuvenates. Proceeding from this point of fixing the age of the Soul in eternal life, you can just make control in the movement to this point through Consciousness and, at the same time, the movement from this point to the human body. You may discover that this movement will be inside the body. The Soul that is in the body reproduces a point outside itself at some distance from the body. It turns out that everything from the outside is reproduced by an action, in fact, of the body where many factors are joined by: the Soul, the Spirit, Consciousness and Body.

The Creator created the entire outside world, proceeding from Himself, from His Personality. Applying this principle in this method, you can see that the monitoring of the rejuvenation of the Soul is your internal condition, which as if produces this constantly. You should just from your thought, where you lay the structure of rejuvenating of yourself or others, transfer this thought into the area of spiritual action and you will see that it already exists in the Soul. Everything is always initially available in the Soul, as a rule.

Thus, you will see exactly that point in the Soul, that area, which corresponds to a specific level of age or youth. In this case, this point is in the body: it can be considered as an area of skin, like a small segment on the skin and in the body, respectively. In other words, you can also see it in any organ. There you can see the contact of the Soul with this organ and consequently fix the state of youth due to the action of the Consciousness and Soul.

The body as the consequence structure of the Soul as though remembers this condition. People often feel this state when they relax somewhere, for example on the sea, or in any other circumstances, a person relaxes and feels some waves of youth. At this point, really, as during rest, rejuvenation takes place. If you just intensify this due to Consciousness and knowledge of these processes, I have told about, you can create eternal youth.

In this method, it is important to note that when you fix a more youthful state of the Soul when you see how the Soul grows younger, you bring this thought inside the Soul. Complete unity of the Soul, Consciousness, Spirit, and body is also a source of eternal youth.

I finish the lecture. And we have now 10 minutes, during which you can ask questions regarding the material of this lecture, and in general you can ask any questions concerning the materials of my Teachings. And then after the questions are received I will answer them in the second part of the webinar.

As for the questions the answers will not be given, we will try with the help of assistants to send replies via e-mail to the emails, from which the questions were received, and which, for example, are not answered during the second part of the webinar. The material of this webinar will be sent in the text version in Russian and in English to all the participants of the webinar. And, accordingly, you will receive a link directly to the video lecture.

Thank you very much for your attention and participation.

We will continue now in the form of answers to the questions. Well, we have received a number of questions. Now I am starting to give answers to the questions that have been asked immediately after the first part of the webinar. And, in this regard, I would like to draw your attention, as the webinar is structured in real time, please try to track the information and simultaneously work it over at the level of controls.

The first part of the questions. Now I am going to inform about the organization of the webinar and, for example, whether you are going to receive the audio recording.

Quite naturally, we will then send the audio too.
And the question: Is it possible to get a French translation? Yes, it is possible. You should just send a request from a particular email. In the future, we are planning to conduct the webinars not only in English, but in other languages as well simultaneously.

The next question, is now relating to the technology of control, it sounds as follows, "According to the Teachings of Grigori Grabovoi we should learn to control reality through the ordinary state of Consciousness. What is the so-called "out of body (astral) experience" during sleep? Is it necessary to try to control such goings out?"

Yes, indeed, my Teachings says that it is necessary to make control through ordinary state of Consciousness. The concept of "out of body (astral) experience" during sleep is a subjective concept, which relates more to psychology of experience, psychology of emotions.

Thinking has a property of various perceptiveness, i.e., the thoughts, can be considered from different angles. If you imagine your thought before your physically body at a distance of approximately seven meters and look at this thought with spiritual vision from the top, you will be able to view the contours of the physical human body. And if you get closer, you will be able to see that the body may be also looking like your body. In other words with spiritual vision, you can magnify as if zoom the image through a magnifying glass, like on a camera.

During sleep a certain external monitoring of thought exchange works. Human thought has a dual function: one function is the exit of thought into external space, and the second function of thought, while sleeping, is the function of creating the body shape. That is to say, the information of thought during sleep in the form of a certain light energy is imposed on the physical body, and the man sleeps as if under the veil of the thought. By the way, here is a good method of relaxation, if you imagine that a thought covers the human body, a person has a rest faster, even if he does not sleep. While ensuring eternal life it is important to be able to relax actively and intensively even when you do not sleep.

So well, the second part of the thought, which is displayed in the external environment, can resemble the physical body viewed from the side. In this case, the thought as a form of Consciousness evolves and at the same time receives information from the outside infinite environment and from the Creator. Therefore, when people speak about the astral body leaving during sleep, it could be just an observation of one of the angles of the thought. This process does not require any special monitoring, besides, if it is necessary, general methods of control, for example, based on my Teachings, and relates more to the subjective human perception exactly of his body in the form of the structure of a thought.

The structure of control based on the Teachings does not contain such radical concepts as "out of body (astral) experience", so if this information causes some concern, for example, or requires additional attention, it is easier to make a control for normalization of this element and work in conditions of the normal state of Consciousness. The most optimal variant of work with the technologies of the Teachings, well, when there is such an opportunity in terms of calm situation; it is calm thinking and control via the logic of control.

If you use any other principle, such as emotional one, it is important to monitor in order to carry out the technologies of control. It is often in everyday affairs if there is some information, like, for example, the release of astral bodies and so forth, man has many sources of information. In these circumstances, it is important to implement the goal of control according to the Teachings. If you do not have time currently, you can work with information of the past, carrying out the necessary actions in the information of the past.

To ensure eternal life it is essential to be capable to create the appropriate events at the right time in the future. Therefore, when you get various information of this type the main thing in this case is to avoid being distracted by it and to act on the methods of creating technologies to ensure eternal life.

* * *

The next question. How can I understand, that I myself have made a spiritual action? How to organize it more precisely, to perform it?

To understand that a person performed a spiritual action, you have to focus your attention on the level of the heart, and then concentrate on the spine, and visualize silvery glowing on the fingertips. Then you should draw this glow of silver color through mental rays to the heart area. And when you do this, you will have a form in front of you in the shape of a cone with the peak down.

To diagnose the exact perfect spiritual action, you will have to determine inside this cone silvery-white glow. If such glow is slight or it does not appear at all, then for the accuracy of produced spiritual actions, based on technologies, it is necessary to repeat it.

That part of the question, asking how to organize more precisely, it is that you should wait until the glow appears inside the cone. The first way to repeat the action is very simple: as the materials exist in the form of texts, just read the exact part of the text. If the glow does not occur in the required form, as a rule, the text already creates the primary glow in this cone; then you should visualize, vastly perceive the structure of the text through visual images.

I mean "visual images", which are specifically described in the technologies: for example, in part 1 of the webinar I described the point, which is approximately three meters away from man. With advanced degree of controlling clairvoyance, this point is directly visible, i.e. it is in the environment as an objective reality. Instrument systems can also identify these points. Therefore, the task is just to direct properly your mental gaze into this area, to this point. The same applies to spiritual action.

In the system of work with optical information of reality, the main thing is the exact routes and exact coordinates of works. And when we have such coordinates, you therefore get that spiritual action which is really described in the technologies, i.e. it should manifest itself in the form of this glowing area in the center, well namely in the cone.

The next question is as follows. How can I determine that the process of body building on the spiritual basis has started? Will this change take place in each organ one by one or somehow differently? Is it relevant to the topic of eternal life?

The fact is that, in the structure of realization of eternal life, both the system of spiritual development and development system for the biological body are of significance. Therefore, responding to the third part of the question, it is relevant to the topic of eternal life in conjunction with ensuring all conditions for eternal life for biological body, i.e., physical body.

That part of the lecture, which I gave on the use of light levels of control, of spiritual plane, these levels are connected with the provision of exactly all eternal life systems of the physical body, including the system of events. Therefore, we say that the norm of the physical body development should be ensured, i.e. the biological norm of the body, and at the same time, it is necessary to ensure that the physical body is provided with the mandatory level of eternal development through spiritual action: the spiritual action has to ensure exactly the eternal development of the physical body.

Thereby, as for that part of the question, which exactly refers to the transition to the spiritual level of the construction of the body, here you should distinguish the spiritual level as the controlling level. In other words, we are talking about the same physical body, which is developed so that the spiritual control results in eternal life of this body: physical, biological body. In the conditions of eternal infinite development and endless development of space, and technologies, the task of the Teachings is to keep, as it is, the appearance of the physical body of man to prevent any mutations related to time and to avoid replacing the physical body with cybernetic systems.

Therefore, the spiritual development has to fix all the time the currently existing physical body of man as a certain matrix. In this sense, it is the answer to the third part of the question, that is, yes; the spiritual development is relevant to the topic of eternal life, and in this sense too. With the development of scientific direction, associated with the wave principle of the world structure, many structures exactly of spiritual development that is required for target development, will be defined in in the form of specific, including mathematical models, physical and mathematical models.

Part of specific mathematical formal ideas of this process I made through the system of higher mathematics, via tensor analysis: through a special direction in mathematics, i.e., tensor analysis. Therefore, we can say that many directions will be eventually clearly defined: when to implement more the biological function of the body, when to implement more the spiritual control to ensure the biological function of the body; however, at present, the methodology of the Teachings practically makes it possible to do this.

The next question is as follows. The ideas of Christ had been introduced into the Collective Consciousness two thousand years ago. The awareness of the various principles: "do not kill", "do not steal" is slow. Well the meaning of the question is what should happen to ensure that rejuvenation and other ideas of eternal life were implemented quickly enough instead of being delayed for a long time.

First of all, I consider, and it is really so, this is a systemic harnessing of knowledge on ensuring eternal life. In this case, I would like to emphasize once again that I teach to ensure rejuvenation for realization of eternal life, and not just rejuvenation. Therefore, rejuvenation, in this case, is one of the tools to achieve eternal life and the necessity of periodic rejuvenescence. And mastering namely the systemic knowledge in this direction includes mastering other directions of eternal life.

To ensure that harnessing of knowledge is systemic exactly in the structure of my Teachings, you should consider more specifically all issues related to the development of the Teachings. Given that the Teachings will constantly evolve and be complemented by the eternal time, for systemic development it is necessary to learn it from the beginning. Then the practice of the Teachings will become clear faster and the theoretical basics will be mastered quicker.

Now for this purpose an opportunity to have training courses on "The Program of the Teachings of Grigori Grabovoi" has been created on the basis of the platform grigori-grabovoi.world . The course begins with "The Introductory Course", which reflects the different characteristics of the Teachings and provides actually the main positions of the Teachings and the spheres of its implementation. Then it sets out the material of the Teachings with the earliest lectures, seminars, and provides scientific evidence for mandatory implementation of the Teachings, provides practices and methodological systems that enable students to master.

Thus, according to the University program the school year began from October 5: now it is the first semester. The training program also implies an opportunity to master individual tutorials. The practice of salvation, which can be used in securing eternal life, is such that often it is necessary to master the material quickly. Therefore, along with the many years course according to the University program, optional courses will be held simultaneously via the same platform grigori-grabovoi.world .

The optional courses, besides learning, also teach the system of promotion of the Teachings, the system of explanations, the system of interpretations of the practical results. Such courses are conducted through the platform of grigori-grabovoi.world , as well as through licensed teachers and licensed individuals and legal entities.

At the same time, by the way, **there was a question** concerning why the agreement offers only the lists of twenty-eight countries of the European Union, Japan, China, Australia, the United States and Serbia? In this case, the training is conducted on the territories of these countries, because there is a protection technology here through the trademarks. Therefore, the systemic courses, the systemic educational profile institutions are created exactly in these countries; the process of education takes place in these countries.

Therefore those who has the licenses and sublicenses, they also work according to the territories of these countries. That is to say, currently, in terms of the legal part of the educational process, much is being done for systemic learning the Teachings. Those who go to educational courses under the program of the University will receive all materials of the Teachings on this particular course, and will be able to learn on a system-fundamental level all the technologies of the Teachings.

With a big enough number of people who have fundamental education on the Teachings, as well as those who have good results even in the educational part for individual courses, who has good results even after having short courses, they will create the appropriate level of control in the Collective Consciousness, and all together they will create that level, which will provide a very sharp acceleration of processes related to achieving eternal life, including mastering the rejuvenation. Therefore, according to the question wording, to ensure quicker development of these processes generally, we need to get more people involved in these technologies.

And, by the way, here, **among the questions** there are, shall we say, other questions related to the subject of rejuvenation issues, the questions of this type: why, for example, some teachers who study, exactly the teachers of the Teachings, do not have quick rejuvenation?

Ninety percent, as a rule, the hampering external signs of rejuvenation, is exactly the process of psychological adaptation. I had a case in my practice in 2001, when a woman who just applied technologies, rejuvenated so that a notary refused to sign, certify her signature, because he could not recognize her, could not identify her based on the passport. And really, when she came, I found abrupt rejuvenation for a short time. She had to bring someone from relatives to identify her personality at the notary's office.

Therefore, I think that herein, the elements of the psychology of behavior are of significance. To rejuvenate abruptly the person has to change his location somehow for some time, but usually this is not necessary and rarely, someone will solve this task, therefore rejuvenation shall be resolved by a preliminary psychological event training of others. That is to say this is information about methodologies of rejuvenation, conducting discussions on the subject, finding those who are fine with this and welcomes this, well perhaps creation of some clubs for rejuvenation, well, in a word, the usual normal social activities to address the issue, which is called rejuvenation for implementation of eternal life. Then it will look very comfortable and will develop positively for all parties.

In addition, as I said earlier, there are people who feel comfortable in a certain age, so let us say elderly age, and perhaps not everyone seeks to look young physically. That is to say, I know, for example, a scientist who says he needs to be in a certain advanced age, but he rejuvenates internal organs very effectively. In other words, each person may in full freedom choose any age category and, for example, be there, or through the explanation, as I have explained already, rejuvenate himself for all to see. Generally speaking, this direction is also quite important, it is exactly the adaptation of the society to the means of rejuvenation in the eternal life; and, of course, it needs to be developed.

Another question relating to technology of controlling events is as follows. The coordinates of the sphere of imagination are provided and what happens during imagination with the sphere of all events? Where might it be located? That is, the coordinates of the sphere of imagination are provided, and this is the first part of the question: this refers to the first part of the webinar. And what happens during the imaginations (visualizations) with the sphere of all the events and where might it be?

The sphere of all events is from the back.

The next question. Does rejuvenation occur immediately on all the events in my life? Is it true?
Rejuvenation occurs at the current time, since it is a process, which fully refers to the current time. And the controlling part, it may, to a greater extent, occur in the structure of the future time. Past time here is largely used just to determine the age, that is, to take a decision concerning the age for rejuvenation.

Generally speaking, in rejuvenation for eternal life, namely to ensure eternal life, it is important to understand the following: it is necessary, of course, for sure to monitor all the external events of the future and accordingly to maintain in the correct norm the events of the past, which are useful for rejuvenation, i.e. to avoid wiping them out in the information of the past.

To do this, you can simply select some useful for you past events and occasionally as if update them, to make them more explicit, like a type of recalling. And, to a greater extent, in order to create all the events of the future, including ensuring eternal life in the structure of events. That is to say, if you in ensuring eternal life, anywhere in control spend more time for another structure of control, you can spend time for this, because you always have time to rejuvenate.

That person, of course, who has the opportunity to rejuvenate himself and has a peaceful atmosphere and enough time, can do it now and at any time. Thus, to begin the active process of rejuvenation from the current time you should first work out the information of the future to avoid problematic events that would somehow hamper the rejuvenation.

Everybody understands that you have to ensure the process, which therefore will not result in some health problems, or will not exist in the future: no threats should exist in life. These are the main directions that should be dealt with in the first place. And as soon as you solve these issues in the control you can safely rejuvenate yourself to the desired age.

For those who believe that currently he does not need rejuvenation, the technologies of the webinar in the first part can be applied and other rejuvenation methods in line with the Teachings, choosing a point in the future where you would like to apply these technologies, and to prepare for the beginning of the implementation of technologies and to ensure every opportunity for their rapid implementation.

This concludes that part of the webinar, which referred to the answers to the questions. Thank you very much for your attention, for active participation. And I would like to say once again that all the materials will be made available soon after their treatment, that is, translations, audio, and links to the video.

Thank you, all the best.

Printed in Great Britain
by Amazon